LANGUAGE AND LITERACY SERIES

Dorothy S. Strickland, FOUNDING EDITOR

Celia Genishi and Donna E. Alvermann, ~

(Continued)

The Child as Critic: Developing Literacy Through
Literature, K–8, Fourth Edition
GLENNA SLOAN

Room for Talk: Teaching and Learning in a
Multilingual Kindergarten
REBEKAH FASSLER

Give Them Poetry! A Guide for Sharing Poetry with
Children K–8
GLENNA SLOAN

The Brothers and Sisters Learn to Write: Popular
Literacies in Childhood and School Cultures
ANNE HAAS DYSON

"Just Playing the Part": Engaging Adolescents in
Drama and Literacy
CHRISTOPHER WORTHMAN

The Testing Trap: How State Writing Assessments
Control Learning
GEORGE HILLOCKS, JR.

School's Out! Bridging Out-of-School Literacies with
Classroom Practice
GLYNDA HULL & KATHERINE SCHULTZ, EDS.

Reading Lives: Working-Class Children and Literacy
Learning
DEBORAH HICKS

Inquiry Into Meaning: An Investigation of Learning to
Read, Revised Edition
EDWARD CHITTENDEN & TERRY SALINGER,
WITH ANNE M. BUSSIS

"Why Don't They Learn English?" Separating Fact
from Fallacy in the U.S. Language Debate
LUCY TSE

Conversational Borderlands
BETSY RYMES

Inquiry-Based English Instruction
RICHARD BEACH & JAMIE MYERS

The Best for Our Children
MARÍA DE LA LUZ REYES & JOHN J. HALCÓN, EDS.

Language Crossings
KAREN L. OGULNICK, ED.

What Counts as Literacy?
MARGARET GALLEGO & SANDRA HOLLINGSWORTH, EDS.

Beginning Reading and Writing
DOROTHY S. STRICKLAND & LESLEY M. MORROW, EDS.

Reading for Meaning
BARBARA M. TAYLOR, MICHAEL F. GRAVES,
& PAUL VAN DEN BROEK, EDS.

Young Adult Literature and the New Literary Theories
ANNA O. SOTER

Literacy Matters
ROBERT P. YAGELSKI

Children's Inquiry
JUDITH WELLS LINDFORS

Close to Home
JUAN C. GUERRA

On the Brink
SUSAN HYNDS

Life at the Margins
JULIET MERRIFIELD, ET AL.

Literacy for Life
HANNA ARLENE FINGERET & CASSANDRA DRENNON

The Book Club Connection
SUSAN I. MCMAHON & TAFFY E. RAPHAEL, EDS., WITH
VIRGINIA J. GOATLEY & LAURA S. PARDO

Until We Are Strong Together
CAROLINE E. HELLER

Restructuring Schools for Linguistic Diversity
OFELIA B. MIRAMONTES, ADEL NADEAU, &
NANCY L. COMMINS

Writing Superheroes
ANNE HAAS DYSON

Opening Dialogue
MARTIN NYSTRAND, ET AL.

Just Girls
MARGARET J. FINDERS

The First R
MICHAEL F. GRAVES, PAUL VAN DEN BROEK, &
BARBARA M. TAYLOR, EDS.

Envisioning Literature
JUDITH A. LANGER

Teaching Writing as Reflective Practice
GEORGE HILLOCKS, JR.

Talking Their Way into Science
KAREN GALLAS

The Languages of Learning
KAREN GALLAS

Partners in Learning
CAROL LYONS, GAY SU PINNELL, &
DIANE DEFORD

Social Worlds of Children Learning to Write in an
Urban Primary School
ANNE HAAS DYSON

Inside/Outside
MARILYN COCHRAN-SMITH & SUSAN L. LYTLE

Whole Language Plus
COURTNEY B. CAZDEN

Learning to Read
G. BRIAN THOMPSON & TOM NICHOLSON, EDS.

Engaged Reading
JOHN T. GUTHRIE & DONNA E. ALVERMANN

Artifactual Literacies

EVERY OBJECT TELLS A STORY

Kate Pahl and Jennifer Rowsell

Foreword by Lesley Bartlett and Lalitha Vasudevan

Teachers College, Columbia University
New York and London

To the memory of Christian Darley (1962–2008)
"Every object tells five stories"
and to
Three artifactual meaning makers
Joy Ingle, Molly Taube, and Madeleine Wanklyn

Published by Teachers College Press, 1234 Amsterdam Avenue, New York, NY 10027

Library of Congress Cataloging-in-Publication Data

Pahl, Kate.
  Artifactual literacies : every object tells a story / Kate Pahl and Jennifer Rowsell ; foreword by Lesley Bartlett and Lalitha Vasudevan.
     p.   cm. — (Language and literacy series)
  Includes bibliographical references and index.
  ISBN 978-0-8077-5132-9 (pbk : alk. paper) — ISBN 978-0-8077-5133-6 (cloth : alk. paper)
  1. Reading.   2. Literacy.   3. Language arts.   I. Rowsell, Jennifer.   II. Title.

  LB1573.P16 2010
  428.0071—dc22

                                                               2010021553

  ISBN 0-8077-5132-9 (paper)
  ISBN 0-8077-5133-6 (cloth)

Printed on acid-free paper
Manufactured in the United States of America

17   16   15   14   13   12   11   8   7   6   5   4   3   2

Contents

Foreword

IN THIS BOOK, Kate Pahl and Jennifer Rowsell make important contributions to literacy studies and literacy pedagogy by insisting that we pay attention to the *materiality* of literacy. The authors introduce a theory about the significance of artifacts in mediating our everyday literacies. Building on existing conceptualizations of literacy and literacy practices as situated in power relations across contexts, Pahl and Rowsell articulate an approach to reenvisioning artifacts and objects—terms that they use interchangeably—as sites of discursive mediation and possibility. By suggesting that objects are "infused with meanings," Pahl and Rowsell highlight a new understanding of materiality that retains the essence of an ideological definition of literacy.

These material and symbolic artifacts matter to the meaning-drenched process of composition because they create opportunities for interaction and listening, offer insights about everyday life, and provide an understanding of culture, family, and community. Artifacts are particularly useful to educators because they travel across domains and boundaries and therefore offer insights into the home-based, cultural resources of students that often remain hidden; they enable teachers to access communities that may not be visible within schools; and they evoke multilingual, multimodal literacies.

Drawing upon work in literacy studies, multimodality, cultural studies, and ethnography, Pahl and Rowsell develop a theory of artifactual literacies that provides an expansive way of looking at literacy education to include not only reading and writing but also drawing, gesture, oral storytelling, and three-dimensional representation (multimodality). Their novel approach addresses a gap between multimodality, literacy practices, and everyday life; it offers guidelines for connecting children's worlds across the home–school divide through text-making. The arrangements of objects have meaning, as seen in displays of family photographs on a wall, memorabilia in a scrapbook, or use of space in a classroom. These objects tell stories, hold memories, and evoke identities connected with their existence. By weaving together theoretical underpinnings of literacy studies, multimodality, visual sociology, and cultural studies, Pahl and Rowsell provide a rich framework for approaching and engaging everyday artifacts as potential sites of story, community building, and identity performance. Through seven rich chapters that demonstrate the use of artifactual approaches to literacy in various educational spaces, the authors address key questions such as: How do artifacts connect communities? How do artifacts lead to talk? How do artifacts lever and create new kinds of power relations? How do artifacts lead to writing? How can artifacts lead to teaching literacy in new ways?

With their theory of artifactual literacies, Pahl and Rowsell challenge educators to consider the ways in which we can create pedagogical opportunities that take advantage of the artifactual knowledge and practices that children and youth carry with them across the boundaries of home, community, and school. Sneakers that are part of a sport uniform or a keychain passed down through several generations can signal new discursive possibilities and inspire stories, as well as spaces to story, that might not have existed without the presence of these artifacts. The ways in which artifacts are engaged in educational settings can open up liminal spaces within bounded places, particularly on the literal and figurative borders of school. By studying existing "artifactual" practices and also creating opportunities for artifacts to be centered in inquiries about literacies, Pahl and Rowsell illustrate a nuanced argument about the mediating nature of artifacts in connecting communities, affording new forms of talk, engendering critical literacy, and providing spaces for authoring new selves.

The volume by Pahl and Rowsell engages the essential question of how existing pedagogy and policy in literacy education might be reimagined and contemporized in the wake of emerging understandings about the materiality of literacies. The authors suggest that classrooms can be interpreted as complex ecologies that are not only represented by but also constituted through artifacts. Thus, an artifactual literacy pedagogy can engender classroom arrangements that decenter a teacher's singular authority, while simultaneously empowering the participation of children and youth. In these ways and others, Pahl and Rowsell open significant new avenues to literacy educators.

—Lesley Bartlett and Lalitha Vasudevan

Acknowledgments

KATE WOULD LIKE TO THANK Nawal El Amrani, Jared Bryson, Alison Clark, Lou Comerford-Boyes, Rachel Hurdley, Sharon Macdonald, Sarah Pink, Andy Pollard, Kim Streets, and Pam Whitty for their ideas, inspiration, and support with the thinking that went into the book, plus all her MA Working with Communities students, past and present, and the Working with Communities team: Anita Franklin, Jennifer Lavia, and Michele Moore.

Kate's colleagues at the University of Sheffield, Julia Davies, Peter Hannon, and Jackie Marsh, deserve a special thanks for their essential support that provided the time out for the writing of the book as well as for their ideas and constant intellectual companionship.

Kate would like to thank the artists she has worked with, especially Kate Genever, Katy Hayley, Sally Newham, Steve Pool, Zahir Rafiq, and Adrian Sinclair.

Kate would also like to thank these inspirational educators for providing such wonderful examples of practice: Parven Akhter, Sandy Barclay, Sally Bean, Gail Harrison, Jacqui Lindsay, Claire Sheahan, Mumtaz van der Vord, and Michala Watson. Kate uses pseudonyms for the students and the families who shared their stories in this book.

Jennifer sends a heartfelt thanks to student participants for sharing their worlds as well as to Julie Dunham, Barbara O'Breza, Justin Fruhling, Courtney Crane, Doug Levandowski, Gary Snyder, Bonnie Lehet, Barbara Tozzi, the Princeton Public Library, and Ik-Joong Kang for granting permission to reprint *Happy World* in our book. Jennifer uses pseudonyms to protect the involvement of everyone in the research, but she would like to express gratitude to individuals who have helped her along the way.

For support and guidance while writing the book, Jennifer would like to thank Cheryl McLean, Donna Alvermann, Nydia Flores, Mary Hamilton, Lesley Morrow, Helen Nixon, Sue Nichols, Sophia Rainbird, Sandra Abrams, Mary Curran, and Brian Street. She would also like to give a special tribute to doctoral and master's students at Rutgers GSE who continue to help her thinking, learning, and teaching.

Kate and Jennifer would like to thank Lesley Bartlett, Barbara Comber, Valerie Kinloch, Tisha Lewis, Rebecca Rogers, and Lalitha Vasudevan for their academic and editorial help and support.

Kate and Jennifer would like to thank Eve Stirling and Keri Facer, our readers of the book, for their timely advice and generous comments on earlier drafts. Kate and Jennifer express gratitude to Meg Lemke and Teachers College Press for their support.

Finally, Kate and Jennifer wish to thank the many people whose input and encouragement contributed to the projects that inform this book:

Kate's Projects

My Family My Story: Mrs. Entwhistle, Jennie Forrester, Justine Reilly, Jenny Wells, the Museums Libraries and Archives Council (MLA), UK

Capturing the Community: Sally Bean, David Gilbert, Katy Hayley, Adrian Sinclair, Creative Partnerships, UK

Art, Artists and Artefacts: Kate Genever, Steve Pool, Lou Comerford Boyes, The Arts Council, UK

Ferham Families: David Gilbert, Wendy Leak, Kim Knott, Andy Pollard, Zahir Rafiq, the Arts and Humanities Research Council (AHRC), Diasporas, Identities Migration fund, UK

Every Object Tells a Story: Parven Ahkter, Abi Hackett, Jacqui Lindsay, Zahir Rafiq, the University of Sheffield Knowledge Transfer Opportunities Fund

Reasons to Write: Sandy Barclay, Gail Harrison, Sally Newham, Steve Pool, Creative Partnerships, UK

Jennifer's Projects

Multimodality and New Literacy Studies in Teacher Education: Judy Blaney, Marianna Diiorio, and Dorothy Rajaratnam, OISE/UT School–University Partnership Grant

Family Literacy Experiences: Kathy Broad, Marianna Diiorio, and Mary-Lynn Tessaro, OISE/UT School–University Partnership Grant

Screen Pedagogy: Anne Burke

Artifactual English: Rutgers Council Grant

Parents' Networks of Information about Literacy and Development: Sue Nichols (PI), Helen Nixon (PI), and Sophia Rainbird, Australian Research Council Discovery Grant

Design Literacies: Mary P. Sheridan, Rutgers Council Grant

Conceptualizing Artifactual Literacies: A Framework

KP: And you also talked about an old suitcase?

RK: Yes, mum's, I do believe she has still got it. I will ask her. I remember very vividly as a child this brown leather suitcase with all these labels on it. I assume they had labels at that time—they weren't the kind you could take off—and mum saying dad had used it for several years, and this is all the places he had gone to—I think she's got it somewhere.

—Interview with RK, Rotherham

OBJECTS, OR ARTIFACTS, as we call them in this book, are present in everyone's life. Memories of objects are powerful pulls on identity. The conversation above describes an object—a suitcase with labels of all the places Ruksana's father visited. The suitcase (which was lost as an object but represented anew as an image in an exhibition; see Figure 1.1) is an embodiment of a lived experience. It may not have value in the outside world, but within everyday lives, it symbolizes and represents relationships and events that matter. Objects are handed down, over generations, some brought from foreign trips as mementos. These objects are special, and they tell stories.

In our work we have found that eliciting stories about objects from students opens up their home experience and enables teachers to access communities that may not be visible within schools. Some communities are less powerful than others, particularly migrant communities, who have the challenge of finding a place within a new context. Neighborhoods and communities hold valuable stories that are often instantiated within objects. If the material world of objects is accessed in literacy learning, more experiences can flood in from outside to make sense of students' worlds as they compose and write.

Figure 1.1. Image of suitcase.

DEVELOPMENT OF A THEORY OF ARTIFACTUAL LITERACIES

In this book, we use the terms *object* and *artifact* interchangeably, but we focus principally on the idea of the artifact. The notion of artifact can be defined as a thing or object that has the following qualities:

- Has physical features that makes it distinct, such as color or texture
- Is created, found, carried, put on display, hidden, evoked in language, or worn
- Embodies people, stories, thoughts, communities, identities, and experiences
- Is valued or made by a meaning maker in a particular context

Artifacts bring in everyday life. They are material, and they represent culture. In our work, we wanted to link literacy, multimodality, and material culture. We wrote this book because we saw gaps between literacy on the one side and multimodality on the other, and then between everyday life, as it is lived, and the pressing need to connect children's worlds of home and school. When a child connects to literacy and is asked to write a story, this is the end of a long process of meaning making that could begin in a different setting, in the everyday. For example, a child could love toy cars and be obsessed with collecting them. This interest spills into a story about cars. In school, this could then be told or written as a narrative text and/or crafted as a digital story. School is one domain of practice, or world where things happen; home is another domain (Barton & Hamilton, 1998). By linking together the material, everyday life of a child with narrative, two domains of practice—home and school—are then brought together through text-making.

Traditionally, literacy is seen as a repertoire of skills that individuals use to do something, such as speaking, listening, communicating, reading, or writing. Yet literacy is always shaped by the social context in which it occurs. Brian Street (1993) describes this as an *ideological* model of literacy; that is, it is shaped by context, power, and history. For example, the literacy found in schools is actually just one kind of literacy. Thinking about literacy in homes—shopping lists, notes, letters—gives a different feel for literacy. The motivation to write is clearer when placed in an everyday context. Artifacts open up worlds for meaning makers, worlds that are frequently, if not always, silent in formal, institutional settings like schooling. Artifacts link to students' everyday lives and cultural histories. Artifacts provide the connecting piece—they move, travel across home and school, and these movements provide power to students. Thus, artifactual literacy as a concept can take in, as its range, the movement of artifacts across sites. When students come to encounter multiple literacies, they often do so through artifacts.

Merging artifacts with literacy offers a method for teaching and learning that opens up more space and understanding for students. Artifactual literacy acknowledges that everyone has a story to tell, and they bring that story into their learning. This approach is tied to the everyday and the "flow" of communication that exists when people share stories about an object within a home setting or between friends or within community settings (Csikszentmihalyi & Rochberg-Halton, 1981). This book provides an approach to literacy teaching and learning by unpeeling how homes, communities, neighborhoods, schools, writing, talk, and digital media are all artifactual. It is an approach to literacy that understands that multimodality is important but also asks educators to think about literacy teaching as material and situated. Let us now consider in more depth some of the concepts that led us to develop artifactual literacy.

Literacy

We initially focused on literacy but now widen the term to *literacies* to signal the way in which literacy is multiple (Flewitt, 2008). It involves many different scripts, and it can exist in many different languages and settings. Stories can be multilingual and can involve crossings of languages. The potential inherent in working with artifacts is that other languages and cultural experiences can be let in. Patricia Sanchez (2007) describes how Mexican students constructed a bilingual storybook for children, drawing on pictorial artifacts that represented the experience of crossing the border from Mexico to the United States. She notes how, in the case of the young people,

> artifacts could also trigger similar storytelling events; as authors and illustrators, the youth decided to include several pictorial artifacts in the book's illustrations to hopefully spark multiple narratives among transnational Mexican readers of the children's picture storybook. (p. 268)

Artifactual literacies takes account of migrant literacies by bringing to life the actual objects, whether remembered in narratives or actually present in homes, that evoke experiences of the country where people have come from.

Our conceptualization of literacy becomes wider when literacy is extended to literacies. The word *literacies* signals that literacy is multiple, diverse, and multilingual and spans domains of practice, from home to school to community, and in each domain there are different literacies. These literacies are artifactual and link to texts. With this view in mind, it is important to look at the concept of texts. In this book, we use the word *texts* to mean books, writing, physical manifestations of ideas. Texts are representations that are inscribed—written or drawn—as opposed to artifacts that are found, created, and made for a purpose. Texts have a more representational quality. Schools tend to be places where texts get made, such as writings, drawings, collages, models, and films. Texts are also found in homes— books, recipe cards, manuals, computer documents, drawings, and models. Texts can be both multimodal and have material qualities, since they contain words and images and these both work together to create meaning (Kress, 1997; Kress & van Leeuwen, 1996).

Multimodal Literacies

Children's texts include drawings as well as writing. A theory of multimodality allows for ideas to be represented visually as well as in writing. The concept of multimodality grew out of semiotics—the study of signs—and the importance of seeing all sign making, or semiosis, as composed of an ensemble of modes. An idea can be drawn, enacted, modeled, or spoken. These different possibilities that offer ways of representing can be called *modes*. A mode is one particular form in which it is possible to represent an idea. Sometimes it is easier to put an idea into a drawing rather than a piece of writing. Therefore, in this book, we talk about how some modes have more possibility than others. This idea of possibility in meaning making can be described as an *affordance*. An affordance describes the specific possibilities resident within a mode, whether these are determined by the material or the cultural possibilities of the mode (Kress & van Leeuwen, 1996).

Digital storytelling draws in a number of modes, including the visual, the aural, the written, and the textual. Because there are options in terms of sound, image, language, and texture, there are more possibilities for meaning making. The shaping of meanings into modes is always culturally influenced, and it is materially and socially situated. This theory comes from Gunther Kress (1997) and his joint work with Theo van Leeuwen (Kress & van Leeuwen, 1996). They explore how it is possible to make meanings that are situated in social contexts but are spread across modes; that is, these meanings as represented in texts are *multimodal*.

If literacy is brought together with the idea of multimodality, texts look different. Texts can no longer be regarded solely as alphabetic print books but as coming in many shapes and sizes. A child's three-dimensional drawing is as much a text as a more academic five-paragraph essay. The effect of new media—digital literacies—has created an explosion of multimodal literacies. A text produced through Web 2.0, such as a Facebook page or a blog, contains both words and pictures, and these work together. A text therefore is composed of visual as well as linguistic elements. By putting together literacy with the multimodal, it is possible to see how a text has material qualities. Scholars have taken up the challenge of multimodal literacies and have illustrated in their research how meaning makers learn quite naturally through a variety of modes, sometimes in isolation and sometimes combined (Flewitt, 2008; Jewitt & Kress, 2003; Kress, 1997; Lancaster, 2003; Stein, 2003). Teachers can work with students to shape their literacy practices in a way that also draws on multimodal representation. They can encourage students to combine visual and linguistic forms in new forms of text, for example, in PowerPoint or in digital stories.

When looking at meaning makers' intentions, a multimodal text also needs to acknowledge what lies behind the meaning; that is, what meaning makers bring to texts. They are infused with meanings and carry traces of their history within them. They are also material and multimodal. By thinking about literacy as multimodal, it becomes a wider experience of not just words on the page, but the feel of the page, the sound of a voice talking, the curve in a drawing. Literacy, as a multimodal practice, is material.

Ethnography and Multimodality

This book is a culmination of studies we have conducted over the past decade that combine ethnography with multimodality (see Appendix A). Ethnography is a way of doing research that combines thick description of everyday practice with a close account of cultures, peoples, and places

(Heath & Street, 2008). It is situated, involving a longitudinal and considered study that attends to reflexivity, positionality, and multiple sources of data. Through extended study, ethnography provides a window onto meaning makers and their intentions. Discussions of ethnographic methods have considered the length of time needed to undertake a thorough ethnography (Jeffrey & Troman, 2004). Since it is not always possible to commit a lengthy period of time in one field, for example, two years, we have found that it is possible to instead adopt an ethnographic perspective (Green & Bloome, 1997) to consider the culturally situated nature of language and literacy in communities. These perspectives informed our studies.

When we combined ethnography with multimodality, we realized that a new theory was needed, a theory of artifactual literacies. What has been helpful in making multimodal literacies real has been to bring together multimodality as an account of the material, physical qualities of texts together through ethnography, with an account of how these texts came into being or were being used (e.g., Kell, 2006; Stein, 2003). Meaning makers engage with text-making, bringing identities with them. Looking simultaneously at the multimodal using an ethnographic perspective necessitates a close study of people, spaces, and artifacts (Green & Bloome, 1997). However, doing so involves a consideration of such disciplines as cultural geography, material cultural studies, visual sociology, and visual and sensory ethnography (e.g., Back, 2007; Christiansen & O'Brien, 2003; Miller, 2008; Pink, 2007, 2009). These disciplines can help to unravel the complexities of understanding artifacts and their link to everyday life in a situated, sensory, and visual way. To extend our theoretical reach for this book, we needed to expand our interrogation of artifacts to include ideas from other disciplines outside education and literacy, such as the visual arts, ethnography, and material cultural studies. The nature of literacy today is more variegated and multifaceted than ever, and therefore to encompass that variety, literacy scholars need to look across other disciplines to understand contemporary meaning making.

What have ethnography and social anthropology helped us to do? As authors, we have benefited from reading the work of social anthropologists and ethnographers who have documented material culture in homes, in particular Rachel Hurdley (2006), who alerted us to the interactions that take place around home objects, as well as Daniel Miller (2008), who listened to people talk about their objects in their homes. A seminal work for us in charting the relationship between people and their objects was Csikszentmihalyi and Rochberg-Halton's (1981) empirical study of family objects in homes in Chicago. Sarah Pink (2009) provided a way of seeing and perceiving, a methodology that opened up wider possibilities for understanding everyday life that accounts for embodied experience. (Further influences on our work are delineated in Appendix B.) These scholars enabled us to take the leap into seeing the artifactual as sensory, tactile, and felt in everyday life and how objects can serve as a link to literacy.

LITERACY AND POWER

An impetus for us in writing this book is to address issues of power and inequality. It remains true that many children do not gain access to the higher levels of academic literacies. Furthermore, many children do not see the relevance of "schooled literacy"; that is, literacy that is about the kinds of activities that are relevant to school assessment. In our studies (Pahl, 2002; Pahl & Rowsell, 2005; Rowsell, 2006a; Rowsell, 2009; Rowsell & Pahl, 2007, see also Appendix A), we have found stories of children's disengagement from school literacy practices. Yet children carry with them powerful ties to meanings found out of school. In response, we propose a way forward that harnesses the passions and cultural experiences and dispositions of children who are not traditionally achievers in school so that these children can infuse their texts with meaning. Issues of power and control are therefore important when considering literacy and education.

By looking at the ethnographies of neighborhoods in relation to literacy education, one of the key questions we address is the relationship between literacy and power. Some students have more access to literate forms of communication and thus inhabit literacy more easily than others. We also draw on the work of Barbara Comber and others to recognize the importance of bringing unheard voices into literacy because, by interrogating how literacy is situated, inequality can be challenged through critical literacies (Comber, 2010; Rogers, Mosley, Kramer, & the Literacy for Social Justice Teacher Research Group, 2009). Artifactual literacies as an approach provides educators with a critical way of teaching literacy through a connection to lived lives and everyday experiences.

THE EVERYDAY IN THE ARTIFACTUAL

The everyday can be strange and complex when it is not your own space or everyday world. Yet a key argument in this book is that everyday practice is important for educators to take on board.

Habitus

We have found the word *habitus* useful to describe lived experience, the acquired dispositions that shape everyday practice. We can include in the habitus such things as everyday routines, household chores, household in-teractions, household literacy practices, calendars on the wall, routinized experiences, religious practices, rites of passage, parenting practices, cook-ing, and sharing experiences.

The theory of habitus comes from the work of Bourdieu (1990), who de-scribes the habitus as a system of acquired dispositions that, over time, coheres into practice and is inherited and passed down the generations. Bourdieu, in his ethnography in Algeria, noticed through detailed ethnographic work how the everyday lives of the people he watched, the Kabyle, carried inherited dispositions and acquired ways of being and doing that were instantiated in practice. He then carried this understanding forward to the schooling sys-tem in France and the way in which some students seemed to carry practices that "fit" with schooling better than others. In this way, he could articulate how inequalities were created, since the fit between these particular ways of being and doing and the "schooled" ways of being and doing often did not match. He described the match between habitus and the "field" where it was deployed as "doxa" and warned that where there was no match, the student often was not privileged (Bourdieu & Wacquant, 1992). In some of the stud-ies we have done (e.g., Pahl, 2008), the space where the habitus was being played out, the classroom, did not support students' identities. Bringing an alertness to the meanings created in everyday spaces requires an ethnographic perspective that can inform artifactual literacies. It is a holistic vision.

Identity

Identity is a key aspect of the work in artifactual literacies, in that artifacts and identities are intertwined. Identities reside on a sea of stuff and of experiences. These experiences are intertwined with material culture. Material culture is portable and travels with us. We have particularly noted the importance of objects for the identities of migrating families. Museums can be important spaces in which to validate their identities and articulate new identities. For example, a museum in the United Kingdom, Cartwright Hall, created a new exhibition showcasing British Asian identities (Macdonald, 2003). By placing home objects in museums, new kinds of stories can be told and new identities recognized. Communities carry with them a host of artifacts, and if we pay attention to these artifacts, new voices can be listened to.

Stories can evoke lost objects. In visits to homes, I (Kate) found that people told stories that were often linked to artifacts, and these artifacts themselves told stories of loss, displacement, and migration (Pahl, 2004, 2008, 2010). When people move across borders, objects come to stand for "who they are"—their identities. These objects remain powerful in their memories, which are evoked in their stories.

Meaning makers infuse the texts they write with their identities and passions. In our work we have called this infusion *sedimentation*, and we have come up with the idea of "sedimented identities in texts" to describe how students bring their own ways of being, doing, and feeling—their acquired dispositions—into writing (Rowsell & Pahl, 2007). We therefore find it difficult to separate the "how" of literacy—the writing tools, the expressional voice—from the meanings that infuse it. We argue that educators need to see what children bring to texts and to allow these texts to be infused with the voices of their makers. The texts that children create have sedimented within them embedded shards of everyday experiences, and these experiences can be found in drawings, talk, and writing.

Improvisations in Texts

One key way in which artifactual literacies provide shifts in learners' identities as well as transformations of learning is through shifts in habitus. This is something that can happen across generations. Holland, Lachicotte, Skinner, and Cain (1998) describe the concept of improvisation; that is, a kind of change that then creates new generations' ways of being and doing. They write of everyday improvisations upon the habitus:

> Improvisations are the sort of impromptu actions that occur when our past, brought to the present as habitus, meets with a particular combination of circumstances and conditions for which we have no set response. Such improvisations are the openings by which change comes about from generation to generation. They constitute the environment or landscape in which the experience of the next generation "sediments," falls out, into expectations and disposition. The improvisations of the parental generation are the beginning of a new habitus for the next generation. (pp. 17–18)

Watching children make texts, and then change and improvise upon their habitus in texts, is something that can be observed, as the habitus, the ways of doing and being, is modified in the process of text-making. For example, Fatih, a Turkish child, drew a map of Turkey using his mother's prayer beads. He created the map using the beads to outline the countries; he then proceeded to describe, using the prayer beads, the various countries he had encountered, including Turkey, Saudi Arabia, and England. This map could be said to be an improvisation on the practice of prayer and on mapmaking, which he was learning at school.

Perhaps it helps to think of text-making as a way of creating change and, therefore, an improvisation on an existing way of life, or habitus (Bartlett & Holland, 2002). The making of texts is a way of transforming the habitus. It is possible to understand, through ethnography, how texts can become imbued with the habitus. Everyday life is present within the texts that are produced. We argue for the need for teachers to take account of the habitus, as instantiated in practices, that then can be seen within texts (Rowsell & Pahl, 2007). In this book we continually return to the everyday, to the habitus, the acquired dispositions that are embodied and sensory, passed on through generations, that then shape and relate to practice, as sources of understanding and meaning for artifactual literacies.

Change and improvisations as they are instantiated within texts, and manifested within ways of being and doing, are ways in which young people stretch the affordances of what is possible. We have found in our work in schools—for example, in an artifactual English project (see Chapter 5) or in a digital storytelling project (see Chapter 6)—that these ways of being and doing can come alive through the use of artifacts in the telling of the stories and the creation of the representations. Hence, we regard artifactual literacies as a space of creativity and improvisation.

Embodied Experiences of Artifacts

Artifacts are sensory. They have color, smell, and shape, and these sensory properties also affect meaning. The habitus, the ways of being in everyday life, can be also described as sensory and embodied (Bourdieu, 1990). An understanding of habitus and artifacts within habitus moves the sensory world into center stage. Practices involve the sensory and require situated understanding of the world that resides in everyday place-making (Pink, 2009). Acquired dispositions that move across generations, such as ways of speaking, gesture, smell, and touching, are themselves embodied. A sensory response to artifacts is important when working in material culture. Elliot Eisner (2002) talks about "somatic knowledge" as being embodied responses to the world (p. 19). Artifacts smell; they can be felt, heard, listened to, and looked at. Paying attention to meaning through artifacts involves recognizing embodied understandings as responses.

Objects carry emotional resonance, and these infuse stories. Objects uncover people and epistemologies. Not having respect for an object undermines a way of understanding the world, cutting off an important line of inquiry. An embodied appreciation of space and place provides a richer and more situated understanding of objects together with an "in the world" appreciation of experiences such as food and visual media (Pink, 2008, 2009). This links to the theory of Lanigan (1988) and others that focuses on a semiotic phenomenology; that is, a way of understanding experience that is located in the body and is somatic.

Literacy educators can use this notion as a platform for rethinking contemporary writing. It is possible to explore the close links between embodied understandings of the world, the sensory nature of place and space, and artifacts as performed and expressed in stories (Langellier & Peterson, 2004). Mike Baynham and Anna De Fina (2005), in their work on narratives of migration and the re-theorization of sociolinguistic space, describe how migrant stories contained spatial and artifactual qualities; they center on objects, spaces, fences, shops, and specific, physically bounded experiences. When people tell stories of their lives, they create opportunities for space and place to be evoked, and within these spaces, objects exist. Telling a story involves evoked sensory experience.

Some stories themselves *are* artifacts, told and retold over and over. Focusing on the artifactual nature of language, as suggested in the work of Jan Blommaert (2008b) on African languages, opens up its material and tactile quality. Literacy is inscribed, written on the body, or made public in tactile and sensory ways for people to hear (Back, 2007). In telling stories about objects, the object becomes realized as material and sensual.

A THEORY OF ARTIFACTUAL LITERACIES REVISITED

What these different ideas provide is a way of looking at literacy education that is wider than writing and reading (literacy) but also wider than drawing, gesture, oral storytelling, and three-dimensional representation (multimodality). This way of working lets in the everyday in that it acknowledges the material culture that students inhabit out of school. It accounts for the timescales (Lemke, 2009) and rhythms of the everyday in that artifacts can be interrogated and understood in relation to the timescales associated with them. By choosing such words as *habitus, ethnography, practice,* and *embodiment,* we are creating a tie to everyday experience.

As a field of practice and research, material cultural studies offer a particularly rich vein to inform schooling. Schooling is already a materially situated social practice, but it is often separated in content from home. By adopting a theoretical framework that sees literacy as artifactual, we would propose a curricula stance that is different. It enables educators to create listening spaces for students, by bringing in objects, telling stories of objects, creating exhibitions of objects, and making new web spaces for objects, that can shift understandings of communities, identities, and neighborhoods and can involve young people in storytelling opportunities. In short, it *is* literacy, but in a more situated, everyday location.

These are some of the questions we address in this book:

- How do artifacts connect communities?
- How do artifacts lead to talk?

- How do artifacts lever and create new kinds of power relations?
- How do artifacts lead to writing?
- How can artifacts lead to teaching literacy in new ways?

THE STRUCTURE OF THIS BOOK

Each of the following six chapters encapsulates a situated version of the theory of artifactual literacies and illustrates the different facets of this approach through examples from research studies. Each chapter provides a way forward for educators or administrators who might want to do a neighborhood project (Chapter 2), increase and build on oral storytelling (Chapter 3), focus on questions of power and inequality (Chapter 4), improve writing skills in their high school (Chapter 5), create a new digital storytelling project (Chapter 6), or teach in an artifactual literacies context (Chapter 7).

In Chapter 2 we look at neighborhoods and ways of connecting neighborhoods through the artifacts and stories that lie within them. We describe how communities can be regenerated by listening to each other's voices. We address the importance of looking at cultural spaces and how artifacts can connect communities—and how this is a way into learning. This process involves using artifacts to create linking possibilities across cultures, and it invites a consideration of the importance of spaces, the materiality of spaces, and how to work collaboratively across these spaces, such as museums, art galleries, community centers, and schools.

Chapter 3 is concerned with voices and talk and how artifacts are spoken into being. By tracing children's model-making, the relationship between talk and artifacts is exposed. Talk is also engendered through artifacts and can be widened and stretched by use of artifacts in the classroom. This chapter explores the theoretical relationship between talk and children's multimodal texts. It considers how artifacts themselves are present in talk as well as how the making of artifacts creates different kinds of talk.

In Chapter 4 we propose a theory of artifactual critical literacies, which combines work in critical literacies and space and place to describe how it is possible to harness artifactual literacies to the work of redistributing power in classrooms. Place is linked to inequality, and the chapter interrogates that through a series of vignettes and examples of practice. We bring together the field of critical literacy and artifactual literacy and look at how place-based pedagogies can help create a new mix: artifactual critical literacies.

Chapter 5 profiles research conducted with a group of high school students and shows how the teenagers resituated themselves into English class by reflecting on artifacts that they value. An object and the story connected to the object, as well as emotion called up by the object, helped each student to find a way into learning. The chapter is really about writing and how a group of students at risk of failing English are writers in every sense of the word and how artifactual literacies helped them to find their voice.

Chapter 6 is about digital artifacts and ways in which complex digital artifacts can be used to harness identity narratives in classrooms and learning spaces. Literacy practices bridge identities and contexts. Practice is materially based more so than it is linguistically based. By looking at the digital stories students produce, it is possible to build on the material, the multimodal, and skills from pervasive use of digital texts. We think that moving writing into a digital space creates a more material environment. These digital storytelling practices are tied to a rethinking of contemporary writing practice. This then requires a process of revising linguistically based notions of writing. In this chapter, we describe two digital storytelling projects with different age groups whereby students created their own digital stories.

Chapter 7 concludes the book by offering a way to bring the artifactual literacies approach into teaching and learning. It proposes a way of teaching and learning that is imbued with artifacts. It proposes strategies that can help writing and can move students on in their writing about artifacts. The book mediates the world of traditional literacy in an artifactual way. In this book, we move beyond situated literacies to acknowledge the "thing-ness" of people's lives.

SUMMING UP: CONCEPTUALIZING ARTIFACTUAL LITERACIES

We would like to propose that artifactual literacy opens a new world that celebrates different sorts of values—the handmade (Whitty, Rose, Baisley, Comeau, & Thompson, 2008), the sensory (Pink, 2009), the storied (Hurdley, 2006), and the material (Miller, 2008). In letting new kinds of disciplines into literacy, literacy looks different. We think it looks artifactual, and it offers a challenge for curriculum makers to listen to unheard voices. To conceptualize artifactual literacy requires an understanding of literacy as a situated social practice together with literacy as *materially* situated. This then brings in the everyday world of objects and stories to create meaning.

Ethnography is a useful way of understanding the situated, everyday worlds of students. Researching everyday worlds requires ethnographers to document material qualities and view texts as multimodal compositions. Multimodality can create a wider understanding of text-making. Artifactual literacy extends multimodality by creating new spaces, since multimodal texts can be collective (through exhibitions) as well as realized both through the digital (digital storytelling) and within simple activities such as bringing an object to share a story. But we take this further in the book by proposing a theory of critical artifactual literacies. We would like to see artifactual literacies used to lever more power for meaning makers. Young people who have experienced migration and/or are disempowered within communities can bring their home artifacts into classrooms and make them come alive with their new meanings.

Artifacts Connecting Communities

In his groundbreaking essay, "Harlem Ghetto," African American writer James Baldwin (1948) explains that "very little" physical change has occurred in New York City's Harlem community "in my parents' lifetime or in mine" (p. 57). From the buildings that "are old and in desperate need of repair [to] the streets that are crowded" (p. 57), little has been done, according to the time of Baldwin's essay, to alter the physical, sociopolitical, and economic landscape of this mecca of Black life and culture that we call Harlem. What is this casual face that wears Harlem and that Harlem wears, and underneath this image of casualness, is Baldwin's Harlem today's Harlem? Has anything changed?

Today, Baldwin's reference to the casual face of Harlem is layered with even more complicated concerns (e.g., gentrification; displacement; globalization; acts of place-making and place-taking). Many of these concerns found their way into my work with African American youth attending school and/or living in the Harlem community. Even more interestingly was a question that Phillip, a high school youth participant, posed during one of his community video walk-through sessions in Harlem. As Phillip stood on the corner of 117th Street and Frederick Douglass Boulevard, he graciously held the video camera and recorded images of the construction site for new condominiums on one corner and bodegas and locally-owned community businesses on the other corner. Explaining to Khaleeq, one of his high school peers and project participants, and to me that changes are not just coming to Harlem, but are already here, Phillip questioned: "Why don't we talk about how some Black people living here can't afford newness . . . new condos, cafés, a new Harlem? Let's be real: people who never lived here are moving in, taking over, and nobody's really talking about race and even class privilege."

—Valerie Kinloch, *Harlem on Our Minds*

IN CHAPTER 1, we outlined a theory of literacy learning through artifacts. Literacy learning is artifactual not only through the material culture used for literacy—the feel of paper, the color of a pen, the complex shifting material landscape of the desktop computer—but also through the fact that the material cultural world *informs* students' literacies. This material world may not have objects that match the prescribed objects of consumer culture; rather, the objects people hold dear might be an old cookie tin inherited from a grandmother or a handed-down piece of furniture. Material objects link to cultural stories.

What is the role of artifacts within communities? We argue they can be seen as boundary objects that cross borders and forge new connections across those borders. The circulating of texts and artifacts within neighborhoods can become powerful catalysts for literacy learning. The key to this learning is what we call "domain crossing." That is to say, when an artifact is taken from one domain—that is, home—to another—that is, school—the crossing is significant. When a child takes a special object, such as a favorite teddy bear or cup, and talks about it at school, a boundary line has been crossed. Literacy practices are tied to home contexts, community contexts, and schooling contexts. Some of these practices cross domains. Children can draw on home practices, such as making a greeting card, making shopping lists, or writing a letter, within school contexts. Students can weave their everyday worlds into their texts. They bring the today-ness of their lives into their meaning making and thereby make connections across the domains of home, community, and school.

In this chapter the focus is on artifacts in homes, communities, and classrooms and the potential of connecting these domains through artifactual literacies. These questions are considered:

- In what ways is it possible to move outside the classroom and connect with communities?
- How can artifacts connect communities?
- In what way do public spaces such as museums and art galleries serve to aid this process?
- How can these processes aid literacy education?

What is the potential for artifacts to become connective? They can travel across domains. Why not harness this traveling to educational goals and, through connections, create new kinds of learning?

Starting from where children already are—with their stories of their objects from home, their parents' stories of survival—can help set them on a journey to a place where they can go, into literacy learning. Teachers can create inclusive spaces for learning that draw on artifacts to open up the "figured worlds" outside schooling and then reel in these stories into classrooms for other children to hear, for example, through video recording stories and artifactual narratives (Holland et al., 1998). Museums can become spaces of joining, where children's intergenerational heritage can be articulated using ethnography and collaborative research methodologies. They can then meet other cultures in "contact zones" (Clifford, 1997)—places where two cultures can coexist. Museums and other community arts centers are important spaces for inclusion and regeneration within communities. How can connections be made across spaces such as home, school, arts center, and museum? In this chapter we present examples of practice that can be used in classrooms and in museums to link artifacts to cultural sharing and literacy and language work.

LOOKING AT THE CONCEPT OF COMMUNITY

The vignette at the opening of this chapter reveals a neighborhood, Harlem, that can be walked through and its story told through images and stories. Past and present images of Harlem inform us of the salience of place for identities. Children walk to school in neighborhoods that are filled with artifacts. Communities are constellations of artifacts. The holistic linking of places, spaces, people, and the artifacts that matter to them is represented in Figure 2.1. The outermost layer is place, as in a regional area of study, such as New Jersey; the second layer is particular towns and

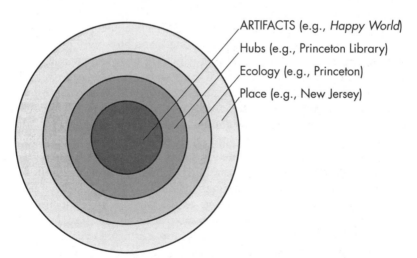

Figure 2.1. Representing artifacts within ecologies.

districts, such as the town of Princeton. This second layer can be seen in a holistic way, as an ecology; that is, something connected through visible and invisible threads that are codependent. An ecological perspective takes from science a focus on people's reliance on resources to access and mobilize different parts of a community in day-to-day life and how this impacts on identities (Neuman & Celano, 2001). Within an ecology, there are hubs of activity, such as libraries and community centers, or faith groups, where people meet and congregate and where local practices and common texts circulate. Finally, nested within place, ecology, and hubs, there are artifacts as expressions of space, place, beliefs, thoughts, subjectivities, and stories that accompany each one. Artifacts exist within a web of activity and hubs.

The concept of ecologies is a helpful way in which to see communities as textured, with different sections (i.e., not reified), defined by large and small, commercial and institutional spaces. People live within personal communities of friends and family (Pahl & Spencer, 2003); they experience communities as ecologies, or spaces that are connected (Orlove, 1980), and live situated within space and place (Pink, 2008). Communities are embodied; they are lived within, walked through, and experienced bodily. In order to understand the role of artifacts in everyday life, community can be understood as being an everyday cultural practice in which people learn how to interact with each other over time (Comber, Thomson, & Wells, 2001).

The word *community* can represent something complex and changing, contested and contradictory, and subject to forces of colonialism, decolonization, and resistance (Comber, 2010; Lavia & Moore, 2010). Moje (2000) suggests that the concept of community needs to be understood not as a reified fact but as something complex, contested, and alive with problematics. Children perceive the neighborhoods in which they live from particular, situated perspectives that may differ from those of adults. Studies such as those by Christiansen and O'Brien (2003) and Orellana (1999) have involved asking children to represent their social worlds through images, in interaction, and through walking around the community with the researchers. Children come at their experience bodily, through their own eyes. Ethnography and cultural geography provide situated accounts of children's and adults' experience of place and space and the body (Christiansen & O'Brien, 2003; Pink, 2008, 2009; Watson & Cunningham-Burley, 2001). Kinloch's vignette at the beginning of the chapter shows us the ways in which identities are inextricably interwoven with place. Neighborhood and the local community are where children first encounter others, and it is in these encounters that stories emerge and take shape over time.

CAPTURING THE COMMUNITY THROUGH CAMERAS

Marg's students take possession of their neighborhood by walking around in it, by exploring its nooks and secret places, by finding favorite places.
—B. Comber, P. Thompson, and M. Wells,
"Critical Literacy Finds a 'Place'"

Walking around a community a school lies within, and taking photographs can help situate the artifactual literacies within a school. In 2005–2007, I (Kate) was involved in a project called Capturing the Community in Barnsley, a town in the United Kingdom (see Appendix A). A group of artists gave cameras to children, who then walked around the community, noticing new things:

> [We were] looking with a different eye, looking for the detail, we used view finders, and they [the children] were going in, and it was fantastic, the photographs that we got from it. Because even though they [the children] walk past or drive past every single day, they were all finding things they had not seen before, and it was like they were really getting into it. (Year 1 teacher, interview, November 1, 2005)

In the second year of the project, but with a new group of Year 1 children (5- to 6-year-olds), the children were asked to take a different viewpoint:

> We went out into the community again. We did the photos, but this time we took it as a different slant. We did doors and windows, so we were looking for the doors and windows and different styles and things like that in the area and again talking to the community, finding out different things about it. (Year 1 teacher, interview, November 1, 2005)

As the children explored their community visually, they also found out about stories in the community:

> They like to relate themselves, you know, to join everything together. We teach them things they don't know about Barnsley. Of course, like some children know about the football ground, they are fascinated by that, and some children didn't know where the library was, didn't know about things like that, various things they might know, and the

industries they didn't know, like some of them did know we had coal miners, and others didn't, and lots of bits of information that they could share, and the grandparents would tell them, and they talked about the favorite bits of Barnsley. (Teaching assistant, interview, November 1, 2005)

The children then wrote about their favorite place in Barnsley and used their photographs to create a magazine called "Wilthorpe and the World." They pasted pictures of their favorite images into this magazine, alongside pictures of their special objects. Parents came in and helped with the layout of the magazine. The children took the lead in deciding what would happen next. The teachers reported on the change in the children's writing:

I found out that the children were definitely more confident and the writing and the speaking definitely became a lot freer because [of] what they learned beforehand. (Teaching assistant, interview, November 1, 2005)

The children then worked across the curriculum, as one teacher reported:

They couldn't work out whether they were doing history or art or literacy or numeracy; they had no idea they used to sit there and go, "What lesson are we doing?" (Year 2 teacher, interview, November 1, 2005)

By seeing literacy as part of everything else, the children had a reason to write. They wrote because it fitted in with what they were aiming to do, which was the magazine. Writing was no longer an isolated activity. Angel, a child who had been involved in the project, reported this:

There's four parts, that's about art, that's about Joseph, Locke Park, that's about Barnsley, and that's about um maps. (Angel, interview, June 9, 2006)

Going out into the community made the children active researchers. Linking up home and school using photography stretched their creative imagination. As a teacher reported at the end of the project:

Part of the thing that stretched them in year 2 was the type of questioning. They learned that to get a certain sort of answer, they needed to ask a certain sort of question. (Year 2 teacher, interview, November 1, 2005)

Literacy in the "Capturing the Community" project was embedded within the wider goals of creating a magazine to tell others about the children's worlds; it was about embedding words within a collage of the images and photographs made from the community walks. Literacy was also embedded within the neighborhood project the children were engaged in, and the children's speaking and listening as well as writing skills were stretched as they captured a wider landscape to write about. The children's worlds became more visible through this activity, and in the process of making the magazine, and then a community exhibition from the photographs, their voices were heard (Pahl, 2010).

UNDERSTANDING COMMUNITIES AS ECOLOGIES THROUGH MAPPING

Mapping a community creates an opportunity to listen to the cultural spaces of childhood. Pia Christiansen asked a group of children to take her around their neighborhood. She learned by being guided by them and given an insider's vision of their world (Christiansen & O'Brien, 2003). Children inhabit two spaces, both home and school, whereas parents and teachers often inhabit only one of these spaces—unless parents work as teachers in the school. This means children cross borders daily and experience two spaces. Sometimes, they also occupy the "third space" of the street or the playground, and this, for older children, can be an important space they can call their own (Mathews, 2003).

Communities and movement, as well as mobility within communities, can be understood as geographic spaces with different pockets inhabited by fellow community members. Common spaces like libraries, post offices, and faith centers are all hubs within communities that have certain kinds of customers, patrons, or parishioners. Neuman and Celano (2001) conducted a comparative study of four neighborhoods in Philadelphia, looking at opportunities that these neighborhoods offered children and their families to engage in literacy-related activities. Their study shows that "learning and development cannot be considered apart from the individual's social environment, the ecological niche" (p. 8).

Communities as ecologies connect artifacts and allow them to cross contexts. For instance, bringing books from the library into a church or bringing a valued object from home to school illustrates how artifacts can serve as a linchpin for communities and create participation structures for learners. Thinking of communities as ecologies has been helpful in our research in connecting different parts of a community and signaling artifacts as expressive of those contexts. Analyzing how a local library based its design on a Barnes & Noble store layout shows a blurring of public spaces with commercial spaces. That is, taking an ecological perspective offers researchers a thicker, comparative frame in which to look at material and situated properties within a common context.

By walking around community hubs, noticing billboards and signs in shop windows, observing different kinds of interactions on the street, in the mall, in the local copy shop, researchers like Neuman and Celano have systematically noted the meaning of things, people, and places and how they reflect issues such as access to information about literacy or, more generally, social practices. Neuman and Celano pushed their analysis further by showing a socioeconomic differential in parents' resourcing of information about literacy and children's development in Philadelphia neighborhoods and communities.

Similar to Neuman and Celano's (2001) study in the Philadelphia area, I (Jennifer) have been involved in an international research study with Helen Nixon, Sue Nichols, and Sophia Rainbird analyzing three neighborhoods in relation to parents' networks of information about children's literacy and development (Nichols, Nixon, & Rowsell, 2009; see Appendix A). This study has three interconnecting dimensions as part of its ecological survey:

1. *An environmental focus.* Artifact collection, mapping, visual documentation, and observation in three contrasting sites
2. *An organizational focus.* Interviews with information workers, network tracing, and artifact collection
3. *A family focus.* Ethnographic participant observation, interviews, and artifact collection

There are three sites involved in the research:

1. A rural community of two adjoining townships, located on the fringe of the metropolitan area near Adelaide, Australia. This area has long been a settling place for migrants wishing to establish market gardens owing to the fertility of the floodplains and includes one of the most significant Vietnamese communities in South Australia, as well as established Greek and Italian families now in their third generation. The community is about to expand because new housing developments are just beginning.
2. The central hub and surrounding residential area of Adelaide, one of the largest metropolitan local government districts in South Australia. This district is predominantly Anglo Australian, with a growing minority of new arrivals from Africa and considerable disparity between the highest and lowest socioeconomic areas. The central

hub is a busy commercial and local government precinct with a very large covered mall on one side of a major highway and sporting/ cultural facilities on the other.

3. A U.S. university town, Princeton, New Jersey, which is situated about an hour's drive outside of New York City. A site of social contrasts, the town is home to a highly educated elite and also a strong working-class African and Caribbean American community who have historically lived and worked separately from the established majority upper-middle-class Whites. In the past 10 years, the town has experienced significant growth and change, owing to the arrival of Latino immigrants (primarily Guatemalan and Mexican), and now Spanish is the most common of the 55 languages, other than English, spoken in the town.

Part of this study involves using technological tools such as Google Maps to chart key landmarks in the communities; to document where case study participants go with their small children; and to highlight areas with less access to information, materials, and so on. Time-space grids are used as a part of the methodology to chart how parents talk about their networks of literacy information in relation to their own childhood and their child's past/more recent past, juxtaposed with where these moments happen in space, whether it is at home, in the community, or in cyberspace. Looking at signs in the community is helpful. Bringing together semiotics with geography, geosemiotics has provided a language for analyzing texts and discourses in such artifacts as signs, billboards, leaflets, and flyers (Scollon & Scollon, 2003).

To conduct an ecological survey of Princeton, I have observed such wide-ranging contexts as Kmart and Babies R Us. Identifying differences and contrastive features within neighborhoods is key to the research, including documenting where there is more extensive literature about children's literacy and development (e.g., Babies R Us), where there is significantly less information (e.g., Kmart), and the implications of these findings for parents who frequent these community hubs. Artifacts and the placement of artifacts play a role in signaling what a "good" parent is, and is required to do and to read (Nichols, Nixon, & Rowsell, 2009).

Part of the data collection has involved visiting local churches and daycare centers. My fieldnotes look at the relationship among community hubs; community members; and issues of race, culture, and social class. To view literacy as artifactual demands that researchers think of ways of connecting the everyday with the material. Studying ecologies is one way of thinking about the everyday—how and in what ways individuals make meaning in local sites connected to a familiar landscape. The following fieldnote was taken after a half-day observation at a day-care center between Princeton and Trenton:

> I arrived at [the center] right after children had gone down for their naps. At the day care, children sleep in an open area with small mattresses strewn throughout one side of a large, open room. There is a partition and then an open area on the other side with tables and chairs for snack time and books and bookshelves on the other side for reading and playtime. There is music playing quietly throughout naptime (which lasts from 1–2:30). During naptime, I sat with teachers and we talked about the day care, parents, children, etc. The teachers and teacher aides reported a long discussion they had with some Caribbean American and African American parents at a focus group organized to get feedback from parents about their care, and parents discussed how they do not want to rear their children like White European or American people. They have found that health professionals and counselors give them information about rearing children based on the White European/American experience and not the way other cultures might want to bring up children. [A teacher] reiterated that families who come to [this center] are poor and have nomadic lives. Children have few resources, and their job as early childhood educators is to create a strong base for children. They have found that parents want information about their child's development, but they do not want to be told how they should parent (they articulated the difference in a focus group). (August 5, 2008)

In light of a series of observations at this day-care center, I noted contrasts between the perspective of White, middle-class townspeople and those of ethnically diverse working-class families. The center described above provides care only for migrant families. Locating teaching in the world of parents enables children at the day-care center to have access to familiar, handmade, sensory, and material resources. The featured fieldnote reflects life in the local, examined from an "emic"—that is, from the participants' own—perspective (Heath & Street, 2008).

The notion of models of parenting and eschewing of White European/ American models in preference for the kinds of cultural practices that parents grew up with resonated strongly with other responses from parent participants (from a variety of cultural backgrounds). Finding out about the artifacts in homes and communities is a way into understanding literacy practices. Acknowledging and incorporating home artifacts, such as a family Bible or prayer beads, represent a bridging of rearing experiences that, importantly, creates social inclusion. Also, communities contain key objects that are part of neighborhood practices that join community members. Just as artifacts open up stories, viewing communities as ecologies and as carriers of important stories can bring alive new educational possibilities for schools that can open up their doors to artifacts from these communities to see how they are connected.

INSCRIBING PLACE AND SPACE THROUGH TEXT-MAKING

How do students connect their worlds of home, community, and school—both the continuities and discontinuities? Their meaning making, or text-making, the drawings and writing they do, as well as their talk, spans both sites, as they draw on their home experiences. Janet Maybin (2007) describes how these out-of-school literacy worlds can be found within school as well, as children bring their home experiences into schooling and make use of them for literacy learning.

Children growing up in neighborhoods experience the textual and artifactual nature of the space they are born into. Their lives are meshed with the experience of the neighborhood, its boundaries and its lived experiences. Walking through neighborhoods, children experience their worlds in a sensory way, through smell and sound and sight. These experiences are translated into texts, into writing, talk, and pictures.

Material culture can be domain specific and transnational (Sanchez, 2007). Artifacts associated with particular practices can be found in homes, and articulated in relation to migration. In the Ferham Families project, described later in this chapter, a Pakistani woman who arrived in the United Kingdom in the 1960s found her sewing machine to be vital because she could sew her clothes herself, since she could not find any she considered suitable in the shops. Many children now play with their Nintendo DS or Wii in their home. Many also have a favorite teddy bear or stuffed toy that accompanies them through childhood. These artifacts can be carried to school. They can also be displayed in public spaces by museum curators as examples of the material culture of the time. These processes help people realize a sense of self and pride in community.

Communities are increasingly recognized as being about place, about social networks, and, most meaningful, about interaction. Interaction consists of oral storytelling, but it also involves the production of written as well as oral texts between people within communities. We want to signal the artifactual nature of stories, how they are tied to objects. Objects are "in-place" and children and families grow up with a sense of place. As Clifford Geertz (1996) has said, "No one lives in the world in general. Everybody, even the exiled, the drifting, the diasporic, or the perpetually moving, lives in some confined and limited stretch of it—'the world around here'" (p. 262).

Place has often been seen as a more bounded, physical concept, whereas space can be associated with the virtual and the nonphysical. Leander and Sheehy (2004) argue that discursive practices produce new kinds of spaces, particularly in virtual worlds. Gee (2003), in his work on video games, pushed this further to describe how new spaces are co-constructed online. However, discursive practices themselves are always open to interpretation. Experience is something that is acquired over time, and people's memories shift as they grow up. Family myths emerge over time as part of a collective memory; however, the myths we live by are themselves constructed in interaction (Connerton, 1989; Samuel & Thompson, 1990). The experience of space involves oscillation between memories of a place, embodied experience of place, and then the construction of new spaces through interaction.

As new migrant families arrive in neighborhoods, their textual practices might change, as letters are sent home, and the family might use a number of different multilingual literacy practices in different settings (Saxena, 2000). They might use English in public school but Arabic in mosque school, while using Urdu script to write letters home but conversing in Punjabi or a similar language connected to place. These multilingual literacy practices might remain the same in some domains but be stretched in others. For example, a family arriving from Somalia might carry with them Arabic literacy practices that involve attending a mosque school and learning the Koran by heart in Arabic, a practice that might be invisible in schooling (Gregory, Long, & Volk, 2004; Rosowsky, 2008). Children might then draw on these decoding skills when learning to read in schools (Rosowsky, 2001).

Street's (1984, 1993) work in Iran showed us how literacy practices could be associated with different domains of practice. In the market, a particular kind of literacy was prevalent, contrasting with the mosque, where another type of literacy, focused on Arabic, was used. The technical colleges used another form of literacy, and these three types of literacy coexisted. Street's (1993) insight that there are different literacy practices associated with different domains of life make it possible to identify how literacy practices are linked to everyday practice. For example, a family moving from Somalia to England will carry their everyday practices and language with them and then adapt them in new settings. The children of the family might have to learn English, and the mother might have to adapt to new practices and routines in the new context. A cooking pot used in Somalia might not fit on a gas stove in Sheffield.

This transformation of everyday practices—of everyday ways of being and doing and acting in a space—is an important way in which migration is attuned to new contexts. Appadurai (1996) describes how migration leads to a different kind of ethnographic representation, one that focuses both on Bourdieu's (1990) concept that habitus is durable but not eternal and focuses on the improvisation of the habitus. Cultural forms, argued Appadurai, are now fundamentally fractal in the context of global shifts and flows, the migratory experiences that can now be observed within urban neighborhoods. Many of these practices are incorporated into new settings when families arrive in new communities.

CROSSING BORDERS AND SPACES THROUGH ARTIFACTS

Students' texts are liminal spaces where their worlds can be deciphered and validated. Gathering children's texts and finding out where the ideas came from in the text is a good way of developing a lens that connects home and school artifacts.

In a U.S. high school study (detailed in Chapter 5), I (Jennifer) sought to open border spaces for students to find a place in schooling contexts. When artifacts that students value, such as a lacrosse stick or a skateboard, were privileged, students entered a liminal, almost border space. Border spaces sat between what they valued in their own time and space outside of ninth-grade English and the English classroom. Mark, for example, wrestles for hours after school, and in bringing his wrestling shoes into class, reflecting on them, and writing about them, a space opened up for him where he did not have a place before.

A classmate, Maynor, a Mexican American, wrote the following narrative as a prelude to his multimodal portfolio. This was the culminating assignment for his course, and Maynor reflected on his first artifact as a segue into his portfolio:

Dear Reader: Thank you for looking at my binder and I hope the section you like the most was the artifact section. Those artifacts were chosen because they meant a lot to me and they were objects that I have had a special connection to throughout my life. The cat food was meant to symbolize the responsibility and the joys of owning a cat, because there comes a lot of responsibility when raising a cat, but there are many bright sides to owning a cat, for example: Cats are very playful and they love to chase things and this is very fun for you and your cat. The paper crane artifact was something I learned very quickly in elementary school. Paper cranes are said to stand for friendship and loyalty, and there is a myth saying that if a person ever makes 1000 paper cranes, the gods would grant them a wish. All these artifacts have some connection to my life and they are the things that are very special to me and they are objects that mean more to me than just about anything. (May 21, 2008)

In Maynor's reflection, the connective power of the cranes provides a window into his inner world. Maynor saw the English classroom differently by bringing in the crane. The text reveals and sediments his beliefs in loyalty and friendship, and so the paper crane becomes a transitional artifact, an enduring artifact of friendship. Text-making can produce new spaces for children and young people to navigate their worlds, and by focusing on the artifactual nature of the text, its material qualities come to the fore. Students placed these artifacts of self into context by writing about how they use and enjoy them in their communities. By bringing objects into school, they extend their community and their community of practice (Lave & Wenger, 1991).

Thinking about artifacts as border crossings brings into the open the experience of family life and how texts reflect that experience of everydayness. In a home/school artifact project, children in a primary school in Bristol, United Kingdom, were invited to create a shoebox to be called "All About Me" and to fill it with home objects. Pamela Greenhough and her team found that parent–children interaction around objects in the home increased (Feiler et al., 2007; Greenhough et al., 2005). Children brought in objects close to themselves and talked about them, for example:

> Andrew, whose family are travellers, filled his box with twelve wrestling cards, two Pokemon cards, a Power Rangers model, two toy cars, a photo of himself as a toddler spilling his dinner, a photo of himself and his cousin at a fair, photos of himself sitting on a large dog surrounded by other dogs, on a beach, on a site playing in a model house, and with his sisters at home in their caravan. (Greenhough et al., 2005, pp. 98–99)

The teacher also brought in special artifacts from home to share and thereby invited the children into her home space. The teacher was able to link these objects to writing activities as well as history activities. The project opened up deep emotions for the children.

> It was noticeable that some of their boxes contained some very personal items— a first babygro, a page from the local paper in which the child had featured in an article on a children's bereavement service, a book called "You Are Special", presented to the child at nursery school. There were also items given or created by other people in the child's family. Karim's box for example contained lists of his hobbies and the names of family members, created by his older brothers and sisters. (Greenbough et al., 2005, p. 99)

The project enabled the children to bring their home identities into school but also had a powerful role in inspiring writing. Some of the writing was strong and opened up new emotional spaces (Scanlan, 2008). The children's writing referred to the special objects they had brought in. A mother of one of the children commented:

> It's nice to show things from home. I think there's a certain bit of security there, these are familiar pieces that he's taken in and he enjoys and then suddenly they're in a different context, they're in a school context, and I think that's nice. . . . And what was funny was sometimes it might not be the things in your own box that inspire you, it would be things in somebody else's box. (Scanlan, 2008, pp. 100–101)

The project validated children's out-of-school activities and brought their everyday lives into the classroom. The project team were amazed at the diversity of objects brought in from home—objects from popular culture but also objects the children had become attached to over time, such as shells, flowers, images, and small toys. In her work with young children beginning to write, Dyson (1993, 2003) has noticed how children bring in the artifacts, films, and daily scripts they engage with and how these are re-mixed and recontextualized in school. These might be artifacts from popular culture, bits of radio shows, and rhymes and games from home. These are mixed in with "schooled" literacy practices (Street & Street, 1991). Many children's texts cross these boundaries—from popular culture, into school, and back home again.

BRIDGING BORDERS WITH FAMILY STORIES

Seeing communities as artifactual requires an understanding of family. Families live their lives in a web of taken-for-granted routines and practices. From the moment we wake in the morning, family life is structured by the habitual. Families create ways of doing in response to everyday circumstance, drawing on ways of being and doing that parents and grandparents have handed down. The idea of habitus from Bourdieu (1990) provides a way to identify what it is that families bring with them, their everyday habits and practices (see Chapter 1). It also helps identify the acquired and inherited *dispositions* children bring with them to school, making it possible to identify the adaptive *strategies* children use when encountering new practices within school. The important aspect of learning occurs when children learn to *improvise* upon the habitus, merging the old stories and ways of being and then stretching them to adapt to the new (Bartlett & Holland, 2002).

A Young Mother Reaches Out

Part of the international ecological study discussed earlier in the chapter (Nichols et al., 2009) involves interviewing parents about their networks of information about children's literacy and development of their preschool children. An element of the research entails getting to know parent stories about their own childhood and its connection to the rearing of their children.

Jessica, a White, working-class mother of two boys, aged 8 and 2, is a participant in the study. She is small in stature with lots of eclectic and colorful tattoos (each one carrying its own story). In fact, Jessica recounted stories about each tattoo that embodied stories of self. Jessica is married to José, who is from Peru. English and Spanish are spoken in the home—José speaks Spanish, and Jessica speaks English. Living in the Clay Street area of Princeton, a hub for African American and Hispanic families, Jessica talked about ways of retaining culture and cultural practices in the home by speaking Spanish or cooking traditional Peruvian food with José's mother. Also, Jessica talked about having her boys at a fairly young age compared with her peers and how difficult and at times lonely it could be navigating motherhood and all of the information that she needed at such a young age. Certainly what shaped Jessica's mothering of Sam, her 8-year-old, was striking out and using the affordances of neighborhoods: "I didn't have friends who had babies . . . so I didn't have any kind of support at all. . . . I didn't have a computer, so I would use the one in the library, and I had to rely on these resources because I didn't have family close to hand." Jessica's story of motherhood is very much tied to community support and to carving out educative practices from the resources that were around her, such as using resources in the library, the community, and the neighborhood to educate her children. Having a 2-year-old now seems much easier because of what she learned from the experience with Sam. When she discussed being a mom to Sam and Pablo, she talked about being aware of "a commitment to motherhood and seeing your children within a community."

As Jessica's story shows, there are ways of retaining culture within another culture, and connecting the everyday with the material is one way to bridge divides. Many teachers have to integrate new arrivals into their classrooms with students from more established communities. Being faced with unfamiliar practices or scripts or ways of being can sometimes create challenges for teachers. For example, Liz Brooker (2002) showed how teachers did not necessarily recognize the home literacy or routine practices of children of South Asian cultural backgrounds in their schools. The children's practices were complex and varied, but they remained invisible within school.

There are also shifts across generations. New identities are forged in second or third generations, and sometimes different generations struggle to understand each other. A challenge for educators is how to mediate across those different worlds to create communities for learning that link home, community, and school.

An Exhibition Tells a Story of Migration

Rotherham is a town in South Yorkshire that used to gain its prosperity from the steel mills and coal mining industry, both of which have slowly declined since the 1960s, and now ranks as one of the more deprived communities in the United Kingdom. The town has undergone slow decline since the mining industry was shut down in the 1980s. I (Kate) undertook a study in Ferham, a neighborhood that is cut off from the town center by a large freeway but nevertheless is part of Rotherham. The Ferham school is surrounded by residential housing; a small park and the local football field lie up the road from the school. Housing in Ferham is mostly small terraced housing and has a Victorian feel.

In the 1950s and 1960s, many men from Pakistan came to the United Kingdom to find work in the steel industry, where jobs were plentiful. After a few years, the men brought their wives from Pakistan, and gradually, over time, families settled, and their children were educated in Rotherham schools. There are now three or four generations of these original families living in the terraced housing around Rotherham. This pattern of settlement is common in many other northern English towns such as Sheffield, Bradford, and Manchester.

The Ferham Families project (see Appendix A) focused on community cohesion and a need to represent the community in ways that enabled people to come closer together. The aim of the project was to find out what artifacts were special to the families, and why, and to create a community exhibition of these special objects. The project was linked to the local museum, Clifton Park Museum in Rotherham. Another part of the project included a Women's Art Project held at the local Sure Start Center, together with a children's creative art project at the local school. Working with me on the project team were Zahir Rafiq, who was the project's adviser, artist, and web designer, and Andy Pollard, the exhibition curator and co-researcher. Zahir worked as an artist and is developing a series of art works based on a fusion between Western and Islamic art forms (Pahl, Pollard, & Rafiq, 2009). Andy worked as a museum curator, runs an art gallery, and is a lecturer in visual studies.

The families who participated in the project felt that they were typical Ferham families; that is, they lived lives that were part of the community, and they contributed to the community. As Zahir said at the start of the project:

> As an Asian person myself I thought it was a good idea to get positive messages across to the general public in Rotherham, to show that, . . . to just get that normal view of Asian families, common view of Asian families, common something that the white population can relate to, because at the moment they can't relate to Asian families, at the moment, but there is so much that they can, and I hope that will come out of this project, that's why I wanted to do it, it's a great cause. (Pahl et al., 2009, p. 84)

As with many other communities in the United States and the United Kingdom, the Ferham families felt misunderstood—they wanted to be represented as "normal," not as other in the town where they lived. Today, when many communities are beginning to redefine who makes up the "normal" community, this shift needs to be articulated in many different ways and through different cultural spaces, but it is vital for the children of families who might not have been so recognized previously.

The process of creating a community exhibition began with the researchers conducting long ethnographic interviews in the homes of a small group of families. The interviews drew out key themes that were common to the families but that the broader community could relate to. These were the following:

- Gold (gold spray, jewelry, cloth)
- Textiles (sewing machine, cotton, clothes)
- Travel (shoes, Pakistan, migrations)
- Family values (Koran, glass mosque)
- Toys (children's, including Action Man)
- Growing up in Rotherham (photo boards and home background with family trees)
- Weddings (case with wedding dress, textile case)

The process of creating these themes involved long discussions when we took the coded interviews back to the families. Figure 2.2 represents the process as cyclical, as the themes were constructed and then reconstructed with discussions with the families over time. What was special to this project was spending time in homes, talking to the families, and finding out about their objects. Their stories gave a vivid picture of the struggle to adapt to the new conditions in Rotherham. The stories connected to the objects constantly shifted during our interactions, and my relationship with the families created an interpretative lens that itself shaped the stories.

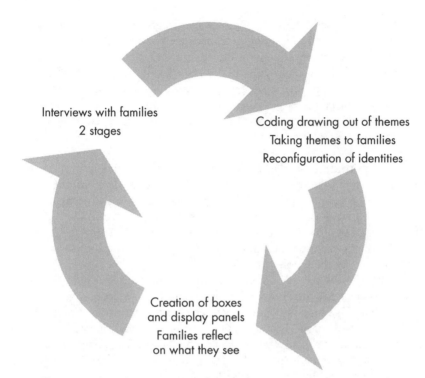

Interviews with families
2 stages

Coding drawing out of themes
Taking themes to families
Reconfiguration of identities

Creation of boxes
and display panels
Families reflect
on what they see

Figure 2.2. The process of constructing and reconstructing key themes.

One family, in particular, is described here. Mr. K, senior, came in the 1950s from the Pathan region of Pakistan to work in Rotherham. He supported a great many other single men who also came to work, and his literacy skills meant that he often helped them out with writing. He brought his wife, Mrs. K, over in the 1960s, and over time, they raised four children, now all grown, in the Ferham area. Mr. K had since passed away, but his widow, children, and their children shared their stories with the project team. This family was very generous with their time and spent many hours with Kate, Andy, and Zahir, telling the stories of their experiences of moving to the United Kingdom and of the objects they had brought with them.

The themes that emerged from the stories about the Ferham families' objects provided the framework for the exhibition. As noted above, gold was one of the key themes. For example, Ruksana, the Ks' daughter, described to me the importance of gold to her family:

As regards gold, culturally a girl is always given gold when she gets
married. As well as looking nice, because you wear the gold with
your outfit, your wedding outfit, it is for a rainy day as well in case
anything happens, and you go, "Oh, we'll sell the gold." Not only
are you given gold, you are given other things in the dowry, and that
is like your part of your inheritance from your parents so you kind
of take your inheritance with you when you get married. (Ruksana,
interview, September 19, 2006)

As Ruksana told about the importance of gold, I (Kate) noticed that the
front room had a gold swan adorning the mantelpiece, a gold mirror over
the mantelpiece, and a pair of gold elephants placed in the fireplace, all to
decorative effect. I asked Ruksana about these elephants, and she explained,
"I always have gold spray in the house, and I decided to spray the elephants
because they were just cream and they didn't match my candlesticks, and I
decided to spray them gold" (laughs).

Ruksana's interest in home decoration meant that while gold was traditionally associated with dowries, for her, it was also a decorative, aesthetic
interest that was more associated with the slightly humorous, slang concept
of "bling," as one of her brothers put it. In my conversations with Ruksana,
she co-constructed this idea of gold as both a decorative, ephemeral artifact
in the home and an enduring, value-laden artifact handed down across generations. In the exhibition, the case featuring the theme of gold combined
both these elements (see Figure 2.3). Designed by Andy and Zahir, with
Ruksana's help, the gold case revealed the many important aspects of gold
for these families—as enduring value, as aesthetically pleasing, and as a visible artifact within homes.

The final exhibition included cases based on all the key themes. Also in
the exhibition were display panels where we, as the project team, described
our identity. Therefore, the construction of the exhibition was very much
co-constructed with the families. When visitors from Rotherham—including
many families from the local area but of a different cultural heritage, including the White host community—went around the exhibition, labels invited
them to share their own experiences and think about how they could relate
to what they were seeing. Many families in the area who lived in similar Victorian terraced houses, but who did not have a Pakistani heritage, also had
fireplace mantelpieces on which they would display china, and many families had a glass cabinet for displaying special objects. Migration also created
new display practices. The K family described how people would send back
to Pakistan photographs of the objects they were able to afford in the new
space: "[They] used to take pictures of their possessions, radio, with his
camera and tell people back home how well he's doing." Objects are tracers

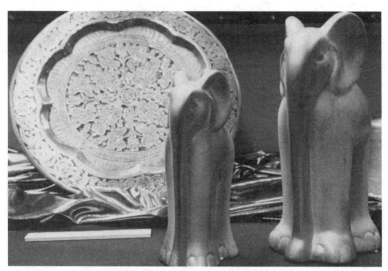

Figure 2.3. Image of gold case.

of wealth, of identity, and this family talked about that—how their father valued the good things in life, although he gave most of his wealth away and was very generous. Objects within families carry competing values and memories. This family valued objects that had no actual monetary value— such as the gold-sprayed elephants, which were made from polystyrene— but symbolized important values, such as the family values that were passed down over generations. Migration provides new opportunities, and new identities emerge in the process (Pahl & Pollard, 2008).

In both this project and the following project, a discussion of artifacts brought individuals or communities alive. In the Ferham Families exhibition, a group of families were able to share their everyday objects. In the project below, a group of schools shared their everyday objects through the medium of display boxes—again, with artists who helped create the boxes. Artifacts were once more the connective power in the project, this time within a group of classrooms. In both projects, the effect was to create many more stories that could be heard and become conduits for literacy learning.

Schoolchildren Learn from Sharing Artifacts

In the Learning Landscapes project, organized by Michala Watson from Calderdale, rural schools exchanged objects with schools in urban settings. This was in an area of the United Kingdom that contained both very rural and very urban communities. Each school produced, with support from museums and local artists, two community boxes filled with artifacts, photographs, and research about its community now and in the past. The schools exchanged the boxes filled with cultural artifacts so that each school could learn about the partner's community. An e-mail dialogue was then set up between pupils so that they could ask questions about the contents of the boxes. One school described the project in this way:

> The exchange of boxes led to close examination of the artifacts by each class. These gave clues as to the interests of the children from the partner school, many of which were similar to those of the children in the class, although there were differences due to the differing social and cultural backgrounds of the children. Many common interests included football, dancing, pets, toys and family relationships, whereas differences included artifacts relating to farm animals and the countryside from one partner school, compared to the religious and cultural artefacts that were included in our boxes. This helped our children realise that all children are very much the same, despite difference in experiences and backgrounds. (Watson, 2008)

As the children explored each other's communities, their parents and family members also became involved:

> Parents were used as a source for children to gain an understanding of their own immediate history. The children were prompted to ask pertinent questions about when, why and how their parents came to live in the locality. We then explored the recent immigration of the Asian community and also tracked back further to changes in the physical locality since the 1800's. This helped the children develop their understanding of their place in both British and local history. (Watson, 2008)

The children in each school grew in confidence, made new friends, and found commonalities as well as differences among themselves as they put their boxes together and shared stories and experiences across the schools. Their experience of sharing enabled the children to recognize that they were a community. Parents, who helped find artifacts to put in the boxes, became more involved with the schools, and the schools became more connected with their communities. The children also had more pride in their culture when they shared their cultural experiences during exchange visits arranged between partner schools. The project brought two very different communities together.

CLASSROOMS AS COMMUNITIES:
CONNECTING THROUGH LISTENING

In the projects above, people found commonalities across different experiences, and these experiences were then made visible and more public. Communities share practices, such as displaying objects in special places, handing down objects, and telling stories about objects. They share discourses and identities, but these can represent differences between communities. People can and do live in multiple cultural communities of practice, but the meanings and functions of these cultural communities differ. Often (though not always) the sense of identity is associated with ethnicity as it is embodied in the practices of the family. Here we consider some specific pedagogies that can be used in classrooms to connect neighborhoods in new ways. These pedagogies can be used to develop artifactual literacies in classrooms where teachers take account of power imbalances, listen and are attentive to cultural identities, and make space for all voices to be heard.

On a small-scale basis, schools can find a "partner" or "buddy" school that might typify difference, for example, rural and urban, or different faith communities. As in the Learning Landscapes project above, a box of artifacts can be sent across the schools or faith centers. From objects come stories. In his work with asylum seekers, Blommaert (2008a) argues that by listening carefully to the poetic structure of discourse, it is possible to hear the meanings created when asylum seekers tell their stories. Hymes (1996) described the importance of place-based stories that were told, retold, and became shaped into a narrative. This storytelling was something greater than just a story; it celebrated "life, as a source of narrative" (p. 118). By listening to stories in classrooms, teachers can encourage active listening in spaces where sometimes stories are not heard. Connecting stories with places on a map, or imagining stories such as *The Odyssey* that involve going into other spaces, can aid this process, as we describe in Chapter 5.

The sharing of artifact stories is also important for creating cultural understanding. In work with students, it is important to honor the variations as much as the similarities. Children can take photographs of their favorite objects at home and then create artwork from them, taking the routine and everyday into a new space. Creating opportunities to move the everyday into the special and valued creates a sense of valuing new spaces.

Teachers are increasingly interested in providing opportunities for speaking and listening in classrooms. Teachers can create listening opportunities in classrooms by creating spaces for children to act as co-researchers. If a child brings an object into the classroom and tells a story about it, teachers can make a video of this story that can then be replayed over and over again and used as a resource for learning.

SUMMING UP: ARTIFACTS CONNECTING COMMUNITIES

Artifacts never sit alone; they sit in spaces among other artifacts, people, and action. In this chapter, we argued that artifactual literacy needs to be seen in context and as a part of communities. For example, the statue you pass every day and the bridge you cross on your way to the bus are community artifacts that are part of a larger ecology that works together to represent your social world. Viewing communities as artifactual changes home landscapes and reinforces identity.

CHAPTER 3

Artifacts, Talk, and Listening

My favorite object is probably a tiny little babygro, this big.
When I had my little girl, she was only two pounds
so her babygro fits her Barbie doll now, (ohh)
despite the fact she is now fourteen
and I can't believe she ever was that small
but it reminds me of her

—A class teacher describing her special object
for the My Family, My Story project

WHAT IS THE ROLE of material objects in social interaction? In this chapter, we consider the relationship between artifacts and talk as well as how artifacts both stimulate talk, leading to stories, and can be talked into being, as students create artifacts in interaction, through talking to each other. Artifacts evoke emotions, as can be seen in the opening quotation. In this chapter we examine how material objects can enter into meaning making, that is, semiosis, the making of signs, as defined in Chapter 1. Objects can be described as "semiotic" when they are bound up with an act of meaning making. We consider how the material can become semiotic, and we examine closely how the "translations" that occur between talk and the semiotic object make this possible (Michael, 2004).

Talk involves the recontextualization of other people's voices, drawing on overheard conversations and other people's stories, and has the following functions (Maybin, 2006):

> Children's talk is simultaneously referential (representing the world), interpersonal (creating relations with others) and emotive (expressing inner states in the speakers). It is also always evaluative, expressing a position and making some kind of value judgement, explicitly or implicitly, on its subject matter. (p. 31)

The creation of talk is itself a process that is like the creation of an artifact, in that it involves an accumulation of different situated experiences of hearing other people's talk and the subsequent recontextualisation of that talk in a new setting (Dyson, 1993). Like all meaning making, talk is always transformational. There have been many illuminating naturalistic studies of children's talk in classrooms (e.g., Maybin, 2006; Rampton, 2006). Within talk, stories are recounted, drawn from other stories or crafted anew for the situation. People habitually tell stories in everyday life, and these stories are performed in interaction with others in families and in communities (e.g., Langellier & Peterson, 2004; Wortham, 2001). Narrative involves talk and the telling of small stories as well as larger stories. Small stories are stories alluded to or incorporated into a wider intertextual chain of stories that cannot always be recognized as "story" but over time can be seen as being the smaller parts of a story (Georgakopoulou, 2007). Storytellers tend to include other people's voices in the telling of their stories (Shuman, 2007).

These stories can be observed in classrooms, as children swap small details of each other's lives, tell each other's stories, and recontextualize the experiences they have shared as they perform schooled tasks. In everyday life, talk can become story very quickly. Talk and story can also be connected to literacy. From small stories, bigger stories can grow. For example, Ben, aged 6, was involved in a classroom project about the story "Jack and the Bean Stalk." Ben had been discussing the giant's big boots, was interested in making some giant boots, and shared his idea with a friend. He then composed and wrote a story on paper about the giant's footprints.

Language, like literacy, can be seen in terms of events and practices. The term *language event* could be described as being "any social event in which language is nontrivial to that event" (Bloome et al., 2008, p. 10). This definition acknowledges the situated study of language and literacy (Heath, 1983). In homes, oral language is privileged over other modalities, as families share stories and create conversations. Educators need to acknowledge the "funds of knowledge" that families bring to literacy (Gonzalez, Moll, & Amanti, 2005). It is important to describe and document studies that look at the nexus between artifacts and talk and foreground their importance in meaning making. Hymes (1996) noted that life itself is a source of narrative and that narrative is shaped through telling and retelling.

Stories can be related to material objects. As material objects are taken into meaning making, they become semiotic. Material things can be recontextualized and can become social objects and subject to a semiotic gaze. They are then placed within the sphere of discursive practices, that is, talk (Keane, 2003). Different modalities—that is, different modes including the visual, tactile, or gestural—open up different kinds of opportunities for different kinds of talk. Material objects, artifacts, create an intervention in a space that can change the kind of talk that happens. The creation of material objects using craft materials offers opportunities for different kinds of semiotic interventions. In her study of 5-year-olds making dolls in a township school in South Africa, Stein (2003) was able to observe how the children produced different kinds of stories when they made small dolls, noting, that these 3D figures provide an important identity function in the semiotic chain. Through their physicality—their shape, weight, density and use of materials— they become embodiments of "ideas" and "images" of characters in the children's imaginations which they become attached to and identify with. They can be felt, touched, held, gazed at, moved from place to place and destroyed in ways that 2D drawings cannot be. It is for these reasons that I think the 3D figures in the Olifantsvlei story project were absolutely central in shaping the children's narratives and providing them with something literally to hold on to in the making of meaning (p. 134).

Stein observed that it was the physical "holding on" to the dolls in the making of meaning that opened up the storytelling. The artifact actually intervenes in the discursive practice and makes an exciting space for storytelling. Once we realize artifacts can become semiotic, we recognize that they themselves are relational and offer opportunities for children and adults to enter into a dialogue with them. Crafted artifacts such as shoeboxes created in classrooms carry the traces of their making within them, and many objects created at home are embedded within everyday practice, the today-ness of children's lives, their habitus (Bourdieu, 1990). Found artifacts are themselves storied in interaction, and it is this story-making we explore here.

Found artifacts have different voices as well. In the Ferham Families project (see Chapter 2), the K family described how, when they came to the United Kingdom, duvets, or comforters, were important for keeping warm in the cold Yorkshire winters. However, this object had two meanings and was described as having different meanings in two languages. The object had a different name in the context of its original use in Pakistan. The word used for the object in Pakistan was *Ralli quilt*, which is a traditional quilt from Pakistan and India that can be used as a bedspread as well as a blanket. In England, the term used was *duvet*, as they were used as bed coverings. Objects often have different meanings in different contexts. The project team wanted to display this object in the exhibition, but the duvets had been lost; the family said these were now in Pakistan. The name and the artifact can also become lost in translation, both metaphorically, as with the switch from *Ralli* to *duvet*, and in actuality, as the journey from Pakistan to Rotherham led to many objects being mislaid.

Artifacts themselves speak with many voices. They can be co-constructed in interaction, and one created object can tell several stories. Bakhtin (1981) tells us that many people draw on a number of voices when they use language. Language itself can be described, because of this, as "double-voiced" when speech is interwoven with a number of strands. Like the double-voicing in talk, we consider how objects, too, can be double-voiced as they are realized within semiosis (Bakhtin, 1981). Artifacts hold diverse memories and heritages. They can create opportunities for a richer type of storytelling. When a student brings in a special object from home, the student can tell a different kind of story, one that connects the child to the spaces of home. When an educator listens to a parent tell of a child's favorite object, he or she enters into a dialogue with the parent that has a different quality. It honors home practice and weaves home practice together with things that happen at school. When parents, children, and teachers all tell stories of their favorite artifacts, they enter into a more equal relationship. Artifacts can create listening opportunities as well as tell stories.

In this chapter, we specifically look at the relationship between artifacts and talk. Educators can use talk about artifacts to create learning opportunities that draw on everyday experiences. They can do the following:

- Listen to children and families in new ways
- Create learning opportunities that respect cultural diversity
- Bring personal experience into the classroom
- Co-construct narratives about artifacts with children
- Help children create new stories and narratives
- Connect these artifact stories to other stories
- Link these stories to more general experiences in the classroom

Through the linking of the object in the home to the object created in the classroom and the semiosis created by that interaction of object and talk, talk and classroom learning can become richer and more extended (Thompson, 2008).

CRAFTING TALK, TALKING CRAFT

Shoeboxes are simple things, but they have enormous potential. They can be turned into miniworlds, filled with miniature people, animals, birds, and other tiny objects. They can become a repository for an "All About Me" project, in which a child might take photographs of his or her favorite objects at home and then place these photos in the box. The box can be decorated and made beautiful. It can hold special objects, to be taken out and described to the class. The box has an inside that can represent one thing and an outside that can represent something else. The box, therefore, has the capacity to speak with many voices. The making of the box, however, is a tool for the creation of opportunities for a special kind of talk that can be called "world making" (Pahl, 2010). It calls up home stories and creates imaginary worlds. In the project described below, children used shoeboxes to create special narratives of identity that led to the development of talk, narrative, and story.

Sally Bean, a teacher in South Yorkshire, designed an environment shoebox project for her class of 6- to 7-year-olds. The children created panoramic boxes designed to represent an environment, such as the ocean or the Arctic, using clay to make the animal inhabitants. The children worked in small groups, and Sally put a strong emphases on the children's decision-making process as they decided what would go in the boxes and how they would create their boxes and the animals. Her focus was on furthering collaborative talk in the classroom. She had noticed that in a previous project, the children were much better at deciding what they would do and how than she had anticipated, and she wanted to nurture this particular quality in the classroom: "The ideas that came up from the children were fantastic, and I think I learned from that you know it's good for them to make the decisions about what they want to learn" (Sally, interview, November 1, 2005).

It was with this idea in mind—children as decision makers—that I (Kate) began my study of the environment box project in spring 2006 (see Capturing the Community, Appendix A). I took an *ethnographic perspective* (Green & Bloome, 1997), which is explained in Chapter 1. Although I did not do a full ethnography, I visited the same classroom repeatedly over a 2-year period. I paid attention to the perspectives of the children and the teacher, and I listened for cultural stories that made sense of their text-making. I was particularly interested in how an artifactual approach opened up new opportunities for talk. As the boxes were being made, I placed a tape recorder by the children and asked them to take pictures of what they were doing. I also interviewed the children at the end of the project and listened to Sally Bean's account of what she was doing. Sally also researched her own practice. Her focus was on a project that gave the children agency over their learning and on creating opportunities for children to extend their talk in the classroom.

The artifactual nature of the project opened up a number of key aspects:

1. It affirmed the children's identity and cultural worlds (Holland et al., 1998).
2. It offered opportunities for problem solving and talk that focused on creating solutions to material problems.
3. It created opportunities for world making and sociodramatic play.
4. It enabled children to bring in funds of knowledge from home and mix these with schooled contexts (Gonzalez et al., 2005).

The children created boxes that represented the ocean, the jungle, the desert, and the Arctic. As the children researched the animals for their habitat, they made connections between their experiences out of school and the animals they were making from clay and other materials. Connor was interested in Arctic foxes and researched them for his box. He decided to tell a story about his experiences in Lanzarote in the Canary Islands and the Arctic fox:

> CONNOR: At Lanzarote, there was these [pause] Arctic foxes.
> TIMOTHY: What's that?
> CONNOR: There were an Arctic fox, and this man who owned the Arctic fox came up to it, and he got into the sea, and he went to this right big stone . . . er . . . and he put his finger on top of it, and then the Arctic fox came and jumped on top of t'stone, and I didn't know what it were doing, and then when it got off, it just sort of rolled on its back um . . . and then that's it [laughs]. (Taped interaction, February 8, 2006)

Here, Connor tells a story about the Arctic fox, merging the out-of-school experience of going to Lanzarote and his in-school experience of Arctic foxes. Although the actual reality of an Arctic fox appearing in Lanzarote is unlikely, the story tells of a real experience of a man with an animal, retold for effect. Stories such as this occur in conversation—and they can surface very quickly—and then the conversation is resumed. Sometimes children return to them, and they become currency that is recalled and alluded to later. As he makes the animal and works on his box, Connor recalls an experience of watching a fox while on vacation. Stories often surfaced in relation to home events as the children were engaged in making the boxes. Carl described his king cobra in relation to an actual experience he had had of the snake in the Philippines:

> CARL: We found a real cobra in the book over there.
> KATE: Can you show me?
> FRANCESCA: We need more red.
> KATE: Have you seen one on the telly?
> CARL: I have seen one in the zoo. I saw a real one in my cousin's house in the Philippines. He has got a real king cobra in his house; he has got it locked up in his cage. He's in the Philippines.
> KATE: What colors was it?
> CARL: Black at the top and steely and brown at the bottom.
> KATE: Were you scared?
> CARL: He went ssss like that. (Taped interaction, February 8, 2006)

This small piece of dialogue made a link between Carl's home experience of seeing a king cobra and the object he was creating from clay. The animation of the object included the sound the cobra made, "ssss," as experienced by Carl. As the children made the boxes, they brought in home "funds of knowledge" and created internal links between their home experiences and stories and the animals they were creating (Gonzalez et al., 2005).

The children also worked at problem solving and tried to create solutions themselves to realize their visions. One group of girls found it difficult to get seaweed to stand up in their box, and they were struggling with how to get over the problem, as Emma explained:

> First we got a box, and my partner was Sophie. Secondly we painted our box, and then we added some things to it. My partner tried to make seaweed, and we couldn't. We tried everything we could think of and then teacher Mrs. Bean had a bolt of lightening, and she thought of something, and we did it, but we haven't tried it yet, but I think it will work. I hope so. (Fieldnotes and tape, February 20, 2006)

Here, Sally Bean is described as having had a "bolt of lightening," and her ability to problem-solve is extolled by her students. The discussions around how to make the seaweed stand up on its own took up a great deal of time as the box was made. Talk can occur where problem solving and learning happen, particularly talk that is relational—that is, it is between children and has a dialogic quality—as children make sense of the world in interaction with each other (Maybin, 2006). Children's talk is where things get done, problems get solved, and they co-construct their material and social worlds. In the completed box, the seaweed was standing up, and the translucent effect of seaweed was created by mixing green paint with glue and painting this onto acetate (see Figure 3.1).

Thus, the artifactual nature of the project focused on problem solving, on researching animals, and on ways in which children made connections with these animals and engaged in different kinds of talk with narrative potential. In some cases, as with Connor, these were stories that evoked experiences outside of school. In other cases, as with Carl, the story of the cobra called up a new "fund of knowledge" (Gonzalez et al., 2005) about the way the cobra went "ssss." In the case of Emma and Sophie, the girls used the box experience to test a new hypothesis about the material nature of the seaweed. The creation of the environment boxes opened up the talk and created a space for telling new stories. Another group of girls created a story about a dolphin school, which resulted in a complex narrative that involved many home–school crossings (Pahl, 2009). Artifactual literacies, therefore, are not only about found objects, already created, that have histories and that create reactions in those who look at and touch them, but also about the material creation of an artifact and, in the process, the talk that is opened up through the process of creation.

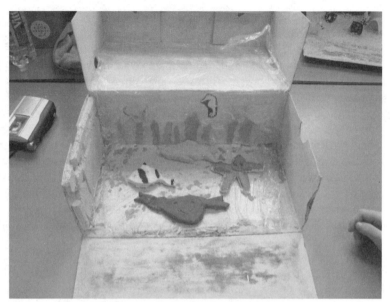

Figure 3.1. Seaweed box.

The talk that happens when students create craft activities is something that remains relatively undocumented. However, anecdotal evidence reveals that when children are engaged in craft activities, they feel safe and are ready to share (Alison Clark, personal communication, March 2009). Many educators who have carried out projects, such as quilt making, collage, or art projects, with students have reported that deep and meaningful conversations happen while students are engaged in such activities. As the material object is crafted, opportunities within the object change the nature of the talk. The overall semiotic output, produced in interaction with the material object as it is created and the talk, is greater than both the talk and the material object. It lies between both and is a product of both. This is because the reference to the object, together with the situated experience, brings more depth to the artifact as it is crafted. It sits within a context that links to the life-worlds of the meaning maker. The agency given to the meaning maker through the invocation of life-worlds is greater in the act of creating the artifact.

TALK EVOKING ARTIFACTS IN THE TELLING OF STORIES

Museums and art galleries are spaces full of found artifacts of different kinds. These can elicit stories, such as of recognition or links to memories. In the My Family, My Story project, I (Kate) worked with the local school and a small museum called the World of James Herriot, where Jenny Wells was the Education Officer (see Appendix A). James Herriot (whose real name was Alf Wright) was a practicing veterinarian who wrote a series of best-selling books about his experiences of being a vet in a small town in the north of England (Herriot, 1970/1976, 1973/1978). The museum was actually his family home in a rural part of North Yorkshire, which is characterized by rolling farmland and upland farms where sheep are reared. Sheepdogs are kept to herd the sheep, and there is a culture of keeping animals. Our project worked with a group of children and families from the local school, which was on the edge of the town and could be described as semirural. The rural literacies context (e.g., Brooke, 2003; Edmondson, 2003) is useful here. Like many small towns in the U.S. Midwest, this was a town that relied on farming and possessed a determination to survive.

Five families were recruited to the project, each of which had one child who was between 7 and 8 years old. Some of the families had younger children as well. The aim of the project was to support the family members in creating digital stories about their favorite objects (see Chapter 6). The families were encouraged to photograph their favorite objects and to describe them. One parent, Karen, told us of her favorite objects: "I'm Karen and, not sure what want to choose" [pause of about 2 seconds] "my dogs, I love my dogs. They are my favorite objects [laughs]." Karen continued to mention her dogs as well as other animals, and her final digital story was about a kitten that got lost in a garbage can but was later found.

As part of the project, the families visited the World of James Herriot museum (see Figure 3.2). As Karen wandered around this old Yorkshire stone house, with its flagstone kitchen and 1930s-style furniture, all evocative of an age before the Second World War, along with the vet potions and instruments used at that time, she recalled an earlier memory. Standing in what is now arranged as the kitchen area, she said that she had been in this room before, when it was a consulting room. She spoke of the vet, James Herriot:

> KAREN: Yeah, I remember seeing him when I was 16 or 17, I think.
> KATE: You used to come here, and he was the vet?
> KAREN: Yes!
> KATE: There's a memory!
> KAREN: And then I dealt with his son, Jimmy. (Recorded talk, January 25, 2009)

Karen recalled that her father had a dog who used to be taken to the vet when he was ill: "He was a border collie. He only worked for me dad. He used to work the sheep. He only worked for me dad. He didn't work for any body else [laughs]. . . It does bring back memories for me. Because I was there [laughs]." (January 25, 2009)

Figure 3.2. Objects in the home of James Herriot.

Here, the experience of visiting the museum, and being in the space, called up a memory, of visiting the vet, James Herriot. The museum itself, full of objects, was a connective point for Karen, a place where she could recall her childhood and memories of her father. Many people have memories of visiting a local museum and recalling similar objects or experiences that they can link to. This can call up new stories. Museums are places of connection, of continuity and discontinuity between everyday life and "other" spaces, and these connections are there to be explored both for memories, for stories, and for feelings.

TALK, ARTIFACTS, AND FELT EMOTIONS

We often think of objects as useful or aesthetic, as necessities or vain indulgences. We are on less familiar ground when we consider objects as companions to our emotional lives or provocations to thought (Turkle, 2007). People's feelings in regard to artifacts have been described by anthropologists, sociologists, psychologists, and psychoanalysts. Csikszentmihalyi and Rochberg-Halton (1981) describe how artifacts "serve to express dynamic processes within people, among people, and between people and the total environment" (p. 43). Artifacts convey meaning and create new conditions for meaning making in our daily lives. Winnicott (1971) wrote about "transitional objects" that children hold on to, that express deep feelings of being both "me" and "not-me." Artifacts can be seen as "biographical" and can be endowed with the characteristics of their owners (Hoskins, 1998). Artifacts offer a way into mediated relations and offer many different narratives of the self in their telling (Holland et al., 1998).

Emotional Significance of Artifacts

Artifacts can become lost, but even lost objects have power, as they are remembered with feeling (Bissell, 2009). Objects call up deep emotions. A group of educators, when asked to name an object special to them, described specific objects such as a button box handed down from a grandparent, a note from a child saying "sorry," small objects such as the band placed round a baby's wrist when it is born, photographs, and jewelry. Object stories can go to the core of a person's being.

In a number of projects, artifacts have elicited powerful and deeply felt stories, telling of fear and danger (Scanlan, 2008). Everyday life can be hard. One educator, Clare, working with a group of migrant parents in Ireland, heard a story of a woman who had come from Iran. She told how her favorite artifact was a pair of gold earrings. At one point, she had no money, and as she was going to the market to sell the earrings, her mother came to her with the money she would have got for them. This meant she didn't need to sell them but could keep them. As she told the story, she began to cry. A male student, from Iraq, offered her his handkerchief. This story, which comes from a project called My Story in a Box, was recounted by Clare as an example of the power of artifact stories in both recalling and eliciting emotion in a group.

In a project called Art, Artists, and Artifacts in which I (Kate) was involved (see Appendix A), two artists responded to the object collection in a museum service that lent objects to schools. The collection was called Artemis and based in Leeds, in the north of England. When they looked at the collection of objects—which included Egyptian and Greek artifacts as well as Victorian household items including clothes, rocks and stones, memorabilia, scrimshaws, old documents and instruments, and artworks and china—the artists, Kate Genever and Steve Pool, responded very differently. Kate Genever looked at the function of objects, what they were used for. She connected this with the way objects were used on her family farm, where her father made the tools they used. Steve Pool looked at what emotions the objects called up. He devised an "aura scorer" whereby objects could be scored for their emotional significance and importance. As part of the final exhibition, he asked visitors to the exhibition to select their most important object and put it in a glass case for people who came afterwards to examine. These objects could be very small, apparently insignificant, but all were tied to personal experience. The project included teacher training, and as part of this, teachers were asked to respond emotionally to objects, to their aura, and asked not to think about objects as part of history but to respond more directly and emotionally to the experience of handling and looking at them. I, along with my fellow researcher, Lou Comerford-Boyes, used this new space to engage more spontaneously with objects. We tried on Victorian dresses, exclaimed at old washing implements, and became playful in the face of this plethora of objects. Artifacts can create spaces for play that are unorthodox and challenging, offering spaces for new identities to be tried out and played with.

Transformational Power of Stories

When artifacts create new opportunities for storytelling, it is important to allow the space for students to tell their stories and become heard. Sometimes witnessing a story can become a moment of transformation for a student, creating a shift in the student's way of seeing the world. Here, we turn to the work of scholars in thinking about the transformational power of artifacts. In their study of 315 lower-income and middle-class families in Chicago and their objects, Mihaly Csikszentmihalyi and Eugene Rochberg-Halton (1981) describe the power of objects to evoke buried emotions and to engage with the subconscious. They argued that "cherished possessions attain their significance through psychic activities or transactions" (p. 173).

They take the concept of transaction from Dewey, who suggested that any act of intelligence gains its meaning only in the context of the transaction itself (Dewey & Bentley, 1949). The interaction between people and objects therefore involves a relational movement between person and object that, in its psychic power, creates the potential for transformation. Specifically, Dewey makes the distinction between what he calls *perception* and *recognition*. Dewey sees recognition as a process that draws on previous experience in an encounter with an object, whereas perception is a process that is essential to aesthetic experience and leads to psychological growth and learning. Sensory engagement with an artifact, he suggested, can therefore lead to new learning experiences. The relation between artifact and person is therefore a chance to experience a transformation, a shift in consciousness. Household objects particularly are a part of the experience that is "home" and therefore they are caught up in the "flow" of everyday life. Csikszentmihalyi and Rochberg-Halton (1981) identify the concept of *flow* as being critical to this state of total involvement with experience, and the object experiences are meshed with this state of involvement.

Artifacts, therefore, offer a way forward, both in terms of the response to objects, the flow that objects create, and, most important for educators, a link to the outside world. This quote below, from an 8-year-old boy in Csikszentmihalyi and Rochberg-Halton's study, sums up the powerful psychic and transformational learning experience that artifacts offer. When asked what all of his objects mean to him, he replied:

> They make me feel like I'm part of the world. Because when I look at them, I keep my eyes on them and I think what they mean. Like I have a bank from the First National, and when I look at it I think what it means. It means money for our cities and for our country it means tax for the government. My stuffed bunny reminds me of wild life, all the rabbits and dogs and cats. That toy animal over there (points to plastic lion) reminds me of circuses and the way they train animals so they don't get hurt. That's what I mean, all my special things make me feel like I'm part of the world. (p. 193)

This wonderful quote provides educators with so much food for thought. The question of how educators can draw on objects in the home and make connections with learning in schools is answered by this boy, who provides links constantly between the objects and the world. His psychic energy is channeled through these objects to the wider world and the goals of keeping animals safe, keeping his country prosperous, and protecting the environment.

Artifacts Tied to Ruling Passions

Artifacts are objects to grow with. Many students have a favorite stuffed toy that they recall from early childhood, that they still treasure. Children also identify the stages of childhood through their objects. Here is Sam, age 8, talking about his objects (see Pahl, 2003, 2005):

> I've always been changing my subject. When I was a baby I liked wheels, then I liked Thomas the Tank engine, then I liked robots, I liked space, then I liked Pokémon through 7 and a little bit of 8, then I'm into Warhammer, now I've moved on from the rest of my—I was getting bigger all those 8 life years. (Interview, November 20, 2001)

Sam has identified growing with changes in his favorite objects. This provided some challenges for his mother, who described struggling with having to replace his Thomas the Tank curtains, but it is through objects and ruling passions that Sam identified his growth. The concept of "ruling passions," from Barton and Hamilton (1998), also connects with artifact stories, many of which connect to strongly held passions and feelings children build up over time.

Ruling passions are tied up with histories, dispositions, the everyday, habitus (Barton & Hamilton, 1998). There is nothing predictable about objects and the stories that they hold, and it is precisely this quality that gives writers a voice. In the following quotes, two teenagers from the Princeton study (see Chapter 5) provide their perspectives on ruling passions:

> For every artifact I was assigned I wrote my sincere thoughts, and put the images in my head into images on paper. I love visual arts and I absolutely love to draw. I'm still not as good as I'd like to be (not by a long shot), but with every stroke of my pencil I improve in some way, and through doing my project I've learned a lot of things about proportion, color, stroke weight, and drawing. (Sienna, June 2008)

> My artwork makes me proud because there are many things about it that are hard to do, let alone be good at. One of these things is throwing clay on a wheel. I hope that by the end of the year that I will be able to make a reasonable size pot well enough to be fired. (Mark, June 2008)

There is a power in artifacts to throw ruling passions into relief and to connect contexts. Objects can be used to think about ruling passions.

Family Stories of Objects

In the My Family, My Story project, as families described their favorite objects, some were very emotional. On the first afternoon, after school, the teacher, the children, and the parents told us about their favorite objects. Here are some of their stories:

> CORAL (age 8): My name's Coral, and my favorite object is my rabbit Floppy, and it is very old.
> VALERIE (Coral's mother): My favorite object is an old biscuit tin my nan gave to me just before she died.
> LUCY (a parent): My name's Lucy, and my favorite object is my children because they are always there for me.
> LAURIE (a parent): If I was to take one, I probably would take one of my Laa-Laa.
>   It's one of the teletubbies [laughter].
>   When I worked at the pub that's what I was called, that was my nickname.

And I was convinced that Laa-Laa was . . . me [laughter].
Because she is as mad as I am! [laughter] (Taped discussion,
November 24, 2008)

The children and the parents created shoeboxes that were to hold their favorite objects. In the photo, Laurie's shoebox is surrounded by her favorite objects, including her Laa-Laa. The box is decorated with pink feathers to signal the positive, loving feeling she has about her home objects, and her box is a vibrant representation of who she is and her playful representation of herself as a cuddly yellow toy (see Figure 3.3).

The museum educator, Jenny, handed out disposable cameras at the end of the session for each family to take photographs of their favorite objects. The families met for 6 weeks and also visited the local museum, as described earlier in this chapter. Using digital methodologies (see Chapter 6 for more details), the families created films that told stories of their favorite objects. The stories grew and grew. Coral's story of her rabbit, recounted above, became much longer over the period of the project, becoming a story about how the rabbit had to go in the washing machine and how this upset Coral so much. The parents and children interviewed each other about their favorite objects.

Figure 3.3. Photo of shoebox.

Artifacts can also be sources of comfort. Many children have special stuffed animals that can be very important, like Floppy, Coral's rabbit. Children have passions for particular objects. People become attached to objects over a lifetime, and they can be linked to memories. As the power of objects within stories is articulated more fully, their sensory qualities also come to the fore. By using craft materials in creating their shoeboxes, linking to color and feel and shape, the families could articulate the home emotions and experiences that made their objects special.

ARTIFACTS AS A TOOL FOR LISTENING

Artifacts can become tools for empathetic listening among educators, children, and parents. Sharing artifact stories can equalize the relationship between educators and families. As previously noted, in early-childhood contexts, children sometimes have special "transitional objects" that they carry with them into the new childcare context (Winnicott, 1971). These objects can be a rabbit, like Coral described above, or a special toy, or even an animal. If educators let these objects in, they can be used as a tool for hearing about the child.

When I (Kate) was sitting in homes listening to people's stories about artifacts, sometimes they paused as they tried to recall where an object was. The Chapter 1 opening story of the suitcase that traveled the world was about a lost object. Lost objects, often signaled by the pauses that happen in a conversation when an object is recalled in memory (such as, "I am sure we have it somewhere . . .") also create spaces for listening. In some cases, a family that has escaped a dangerous situation may not have a lot of objects, but they will carry stories with them. These stories can still be told and heard.

In assessment contexts, listening methodologies can be used to chart progress. Carr (2001) offers a powerful tool to chart the learning that can take place in visual ways, such as using video and drawings to chart change. Clark, Kjorholt, and Moss (2005) outline the different ways they have worked with young children to elicit their stories and their responses to experience. These can include the use of photographs as well as active listening methodologies to hear children's stories. In the My Family, My Story project, I (Kate) used the listening that took place as evidence of the increased interaction of and improved communication between family members. Stories expanded over time. Children listened to adults' stories, and adults listened to children. The digital equipment became a tool for listening that opened up new stories that children could hear from their parents.

Listening using digital artifacts pays attention to everyday practice. Telling stories to the camera requires attention, and parents and children and siblings can listen to each other and hear stories that they can tell and retell. Families hold shared repertoires of narratives and practices that can be drawn on by educators in other settings. Children's stories can cross sites and modalities; they can be instantiated in drawings, models, paintings, gesture, and film. Part of the task of being an educator is to capture these moments of meaning making and trace where they came from, to ask for more context, and to do that involves listening more closely to what children say about their worlds. Sharing artifact stories is one good way to start an artifact project. Another method that is useful for creating storytelling opportunities is to have children create something artifactual and let the stories flow from there.

SUMMING UP: ARTIFACTS, TALK, AND LISTENING

Artifacts come alive in interaction. Artifacts create a pedagogical space that invites sustained meaning making, a web of activity that includes talking, listening, crafting, cutting, drawing, gluing. They can be used by educators to start a discussion that can open up new spaces in the classroom. Kathy Schultz (2003) has described how listening is also a way of creating more equitable learning spaces. In the work described above, talk was created through craft opportunities, through a digital storytelling project involving museum visits, and through a group of artists asking educators to react to objects in emotional ways. Objects can call up many emotions; as educators, we have to handle these emotional responses with care. Some objects are more powerful than others. In the next chapter, the power of objects to unlock new stories and engage in a critical engagement in literacy is explored further.

Artifactual Critical Literacies

I thought it was good that we were talking about the objects—
what we held precious were such random things like an old tin
of my nan's and it was the memories. Also, it's nice for them [the
children] to know that such precious things, everyday objects—it's
the meanings and the feelings that are with the objects, not necessarily expensive things from consumer culture or material culture.
—Comment, Valerie, My Family, My Story

ARTIFACTS GIVE POWER to meaning makers. They can leverage
power for learners, particularly learners who feel at the margins of formal
schooling. In this chapter we explore the power of the artifact to develop critical literacy skills. A critical literacy perspective takes as its starting point an
interrogation of the mechanisms of social control that create deep inequalities
in our societies. Critical literacy directly engages with, and interrogates, concepts of social justice and the design of socially just spaces for learning. Critical literacy pedagogies acknowledge the political and ideological nature of
literacy. These approaches recognize that literacies are social practices, bound
up with issues of power and social control (Janks, 2000, 2010; Street, 1984).

A critical literacy pedagogy looks at the content of texts and then beyond to consider where they are situated. Involving the process of unravel-
ing layers of power within texts, a critical literacy perspective works well
with artifactual literacy to create opportunities to interrogate objects and
texts to expand equal learning spaces. This chapter presents artifactual literacy as a critical literacy approach by defining critical literacy, exploring
inequality in space and place, and providing some case studies showing artifactual critical literacy as a way to offset inequalities and deficits.

DEFINING CRITICAL LITERACY

Critical literacy education is in-place; that is, it accounts for place and space
in its methodology. In their work for the Literacy for Social Justice Teacher

Research Group, Rebecca Rogers and colleagues (2009) created a community of educators committed to the concept of designing socially just learning spaces. Their vision focused on the idea of fostering dialogue and creating listening spaces that can address issues both within teaching and in the community (Rogers et al., 2009). This way of working moves out of the spaces of the classroom into the connective spaces of the community. Barbara Comber (2010) worked in a collaborative way with teachers within the tradition of critical literacy in order to focus on place-based pedagogies, to develop what she describes, based on the work of Gruenewald (2003), as a "critical pedagogy of place" (p. 45). This approach focuses outward from schools into the complex and contradictory spaces of communities, with a focus on social justice and visions of change. Children published writing and art to articulate a vision for the communities they inhabited. Students mapped their communities and created multimodal texts that presented alternative visions of what their school, the surrounding areas, and the play spaces could look like (Comber, 2010). These projects were profoundly rooted in the place and space in which the school was situated as well as the new challenges of climate change and the need for sustainable literacies. By bringing artifactual literacies together with place-based pedagogy, together with an understanding of the realities of inequality within communities, a more situated model of critical literacies is born, one that is both artifactual and place-based.

Critical literacy has also been associated with focusing on texts and looking at power as manifested within textual practice. Muspratt, Luke, and Freebody (1997), in their four-resources model, showed how this could be done with a focus on texts as a source of power. They identified four approaches to frame texts: code breaker (reading and decoding text); meaning maker (understanding meanings in texts); text user (investigating what the texts does and how it does it—design and content issues); and, perhaps the most important piece of their framework, text critic (critically framing text content and design). The framework shifts the focus from normative model to an examination of a range of models and repertoires of practice that accompany such a model. The four-resources model can be applied to artifactual literacy as a way of interrogating artifacts, including their content and design.

This text-based approach to critical literacy can then be taken out of the classroom into communities. This is what Comber (2010) and Rogers and colleagues (2009) have done, in that they advocate a focus on critical inquiry and analysis in order to create a problem-solving inclusive space within classrooms and communities that can shift and sustain change. Rogers and colleagues (2009) focused particularly on the notion of teacher inquiry, whereby a circle of change, involving questioning, considering data, and then creating new kinds of questions, can emerge. This kind of process model relies on a much wider notion of text and a multiplicity of responses to these texts.

Comber (2010) presents a project, called Learnscapes, based in a school, where students look at environmental impact. To explore this theme, the students design multimodal texts as well as engage with real-life artifacts such as a bird hide. These projects were profoundly rooted in the place and space in which the school was situated as well as the new challenges of climate change and the need for sustainable literacies. In one of the examples, a school where a number of sustainable literacy projects were taking place, Comber emphasized the artifactual nature of the project, as evidenced in the "non-school like features" which were manifested in the material:

> Interestingly this school has many non-school like features, the chook shed, the trading table, the outside classroom, the half-made bird hide, the woodpile, the gallery of student work on outdoor surfaces and fences, ribbons keeping people out of a natural scrub area under regeneration. (p. 54)

In her work with schools, the situated nature of the work comes to the fore, and it is through artifacts and real, everyday objects that this situated-ness is brought fully alive. By bringing artifactual literacies together with place-based pedagogy, as well as an understanding of the realities of inequality within communities, a more *situated* model of critical literacies is born, one that is both artifactual *and* place-based. This form of critical literacy is active, questioning, and directly concerned with social change. This project combines a focus on environmental communicative practices with a multiliteracies perspective; it also incorporates the idea of students as active designers of meaning and environmental campaigners in a situated, place-infused context. Comber (2010) describes this approach as one of "critical multiliteracies."

Multiliteracies is a recognized pedagogy based on the concept of re-defining literacy for the new media age (Kress, 2003). The multiliteracies approach has its origins in the mid-1990s, when a group of scholars gathered to discuss ways of reconciling "the increasing salience of cultural and linguistic diversity" with "the multiplicity of communicational channels and media" (Cope & Kalantzis, 2000, p. 5). The New London Group, as they came to be known, focused on the creation of texts as a way forward for a critical literacy education with the concepts of *situated practice, overt instruction, critical framing,* and *transformed practice.* The multiliteracies pedagogy is based on the notions of design, available design, and redesign as core concepts. Thinking artifactually, in this book, we see multiliteracies as complementary to embedding the artifactual in teaching and learning. That is, the multiliteracies argument rests on a belief that "meaning is made in ways that are increasingly multimodal" and, as such, "there cannot be one set of standards or skills that constitutes the ends of literacy" (p. 6). Similarly, artifactual literacy builds on the multimodal as enfolding and unfolding other cultures and stories of objects as tied to experience.

Both Rogers and colleagues (2009) and Comber (2010) suggest an approach that calls for action, advocacy, and social change. This is the approach that was taken in the Ferham Families project described in Chapter 2, in that the exhibition was designed to provoke a shift in understanding of a particular community. From conducting a series of interviews with families, to creating an exhibition and a website, the project sought to combat local cultures of indifference and racism through positive representations of migrant communities. Social change through an artifactual critical literacy approach is therefore both textual, building on community literacy practices and an understanding of multiliteracies, and rooted in the social change processes that can occur through community arts projects and the connecting power of these projects to lever shifts in identities.

RECOGNIZING INEQUALITIES OF PLACE AND SPACE

In the United States and other countries, a predominately neoliberal agenda and overreliance on corrupted banking practices together with the collapse of old industries, such as the automobile industry in Detroit, have created a financial crisis. Working-class neighborhoods have been decimated by job losses. In the UK, the closing down of the mining industry and subsequent job losses has also meant a concomitant loss of industrial-related and manufacturing jobs and a move into the service industry that has also more recently been put under immense strain by the crisis in the financial markets. This has implications for identity narratives within communities. Neoliberalism—an ideology that suggests that the marketplace is most important when making decisions about where people should live and how neighborhoods should be constituted—has shaped communities in the United States and other Western countries. This has had consequences for notions of identity. We have found the literature on rural literacies useful—in particular, the work of Corbett (2007), Edmondson (2003), and Brooke (2003)—in looking at communities where there are dilemmas for both those who choose to stay and those who move away. Moving to where the work is can have fragmenting effects in communities that are connected in more felt ways to place and space.

Corbett (2007) described how these moves resulted in shifts in identity construction. Sociologists have considered ways in which this neoliberal agenda has shaped identities. Giddens (1991) argues that identities have become more reflexive, as people are able to navigate new spaces in new ways. However, it could be argued that these reflexive, reflective identities, which offer a multiplicity of choices as to which identities are possible, are only realizable in spaces where there are ways of experiencing choice. While Giddens sees identity as a modernist project, Bauman (2000) sees identities as much more transient and postmodern. Identities are subjectively realized and are fragmented and dispersed. However, a postmodern notion of identity implies a choice. In poor neighborhoods, it is hard to have a choice when there is little to choose from. Gruenewald (2003) and Comber (2010) have argued that place-based pedagogies take account of these inequalities and that, through drawing on a reflexive pedagogy of place, change is possible. However, the constraints of place—the difficulties of poor transport links and inadequate access to fresh food and libraries—inhibit possibilities for change. A vision of identities that enables new ways of being and doing is only possible when you have transport systems to get you out of where you are. Leaving a community can also have hidden consequences for identities. Corbett's (2007) work reminds us that education comes at a price, which means leaving the place you are in. The sociology of Sennett and Cobb (1973), who talk of the "hidden injuries of class," is useful in analyzing how some people carry the traces of their experience of social class within them. For example, Hicks (2002), in her study of Appalachian White working-class families, describes how these hidden injuries shape the literacy trajectories of the girls she studied. The experience of those individuals who have migrated from somewhere else is bound up with these dilemmas.

In today's world, migration is both a survival mechanism and a global necessity as people move from war zones to better their family and to develop new ways of accessing education and a livelihood. Appadurai (1996) argued that these migratory experiences shape identities, making both the transformation of the habitus and new adaptations possible. When people migrate, they carry with them the sedimented identity narratives that shaped their lives in their former country. Here, we would propose a theory of identity that both acknowledges the past—the "sedimented identities" that people carry with them—and offers a potential for transformation, which can then move people across diasporas into new spaces. A Somali woman who has fled a war-torn country, then finds herself in a Westernized culture, needs to both cherish her Islamic cultural heritage and enable her children to learn in the schools where they are registered. She needs to navigate the new school system and find out how this system works and how she can enable them to succeed in this new space. How can the children of this woman learn to read and write in a way that both acknowledges their cultural heritage and then transforms these identities into new spaces for learning?

In some communities and neighborhoods, children may experience racism and families may struggle to survive; therefore, in our accounts we focus on ways to create space for families to share stories that can create global connections across contexts. We draw on work by Lavia and Moore (2010), Gruenewald (2003), and Tuhiwai Smith (1999), who argue for the importance of decolonizing methodologies—and from there to a process of decolonizing community contexts, in particular, and creating radical, transformative spaces for learning. In this we connect with researchers in critical literacy contexts—such as Blackburn and Clark (2007), Comber (2010), and Rogers and colleagues (2009)—who interrogate power structures and acknowledge the lived experiences of students in relation to structures of power and domination.

The perspective from which a community is viewed affects the sense of its space. Children grow up and observe their neighborhoods and communities. Their visions of place and space might not be the same as those of adults, as they encounter their social worlds from a different perspective (Orellana, 1999). We argue that children's experiences of neighborhood means that place, too, is always shifting, as artifacts and experience are rolled up into new life trajectories and experiences. Children walk through the neighborhood, and as they grow older, their experience of place shifts. From looking at the world when sitting in a stroller, children then walk holding an adult's hands through the mall, experiencing the place-shaped literacies around them. Tim Ingold (2007) talks about "entangled" pathways; that is, he focuses on the making of routes in the sensory experiences of place. Sarah Pink (2009) has described ways in which places can be sensed through participation in practices such as walking, eating, and sharing chores and routines. Place is experienced bodily, and the mapping of place through audio and visual methods—such as recordings, video cameras, and photography—can call up memories of place that can be collectively shared in classrooms. These sensory evocations of place are powerful tools for literacy learning.

ENGAGING WITH CRITICAL PEDAGOGIES OF PLACE

How is it possible to create collective representations of place and space that can become classroom projects? One answer lies in the idea of social space as a co-constructed space. Here we look at the concept of "social space" as articulated by Lefebvre (1991), who argued for the maintaining of shared social spaces as being essential for effective communities. He distinguished between "perceived space," which is produced in social practices, and "conceived space," which is constructed by ideology, such as a curriculum or a school space. Between these two kinds of space he places the concept of "lived space," which is experienced passively in everyday contexts but can become space that imagination seeks to change (Leander & Sheehy, 2004; Lefebvre, 1991). In his work on social space, Lefebvre places space and material production together and then links both to the production of meaning. By linking the concept of space with material production and then moving into creativity, Lefebvre links everyday life, material culture, and text-making together. Collective social space is a space that can be peopled by artifacts and stories, such as this blanket box that holds a family's memories as well as the actual objects within it: "We have the 'blanket box' in my basement. The blanket box is our family heirloom. It contains photo albums, baby books, marriage licenses, death certificates, a mayonnaise jar full of hand written recipes, and a ton of stories" (Wilhelm, 2003, p. 87).

By telling different kinds of stories in community contexts, communities themselves can change through the collective representation of these stories. Museum educators argue that museums offer a collective social space where these visions can be realized and identities reconfigured (Bennett, 2005). Gruenewald (2003) stresses the importance of people telling their own stories and linking these together in order to knit communities together. We argue that cultural artifacts—that is, objects, symbols, narratives, or images inscribed by the collective attribution of meaning (Bartlett, 2005)—can help transform communities if they are brought together in social space and collectively experienced. Public story sharing is a way in which changes can be witnessed. Narratives are sites where people can transform and experience social space. As Holland and colleagues (1998) argue, people carry their narratives with them and experiences constantly change. As children grow up, they create new improvisations that represent the new identities of the next generation. Places "gather things in their midst," says Casey (1996, p. 24). People traverse through place in their daily lives, and they are linked to objects and experiences. This formulation helps us in "understanding places as experiential, gathering processes and as identifiable" (Pink, 2008, p. 179). Places are always experienced and always change. Regeneration of communities brings changes—most welcome, some unwelcome—as housing and roads are moved around. People then experience this change in embodied ways.

LINKING PLACE-BASED EDUCATION AND
ARTIFACTUAL CRITICAL LITERACIES

Studies of urban neighborhoods in the United States (e.g., Lipman, 2008) have shown that being born into a poor neighborhood has implications for literacy learning. Having a commitment to social justice requires an understanding of the constraints and affordances of place. Here we argue for the need to focus on communities that are neither heard nor seen in our societies and on their sociocultural practices that then can inform literacy learning (Lee, 2008). These practices are entwined within material culture— food, photographs, carpets, and other material artifacts within the home that enshrine family stories and cultures.

Children's artifacts also can raise issues concerning power and ideology. Their artifacts are present within homes, including television characters, toys, video games, and other digital artifacts. An artifactual approach to literacy can open up ways of acknowledging the lived lives of the children we teach (Comber, 2010; Gruenewald, 2003). It is also important to acknowledge, as Bartlett (2005) does, that "artifacts themselves are not innocent, but instead are situated in relations of power" (p. 5). Anne Haas Dyson (2003) discusses the way in which young children appropriate superhero characters as cultural artifacts; however, these artifacts are themselves situated within power relations and within ideologies. Yet cultural artifacts can be seen as transformative. Dyson's work shows how children mediate and remediate scripts from popular cultural tales that can contain images and narratives of oppression. Girls, in particular, can remain caught up in images that objectify them. In many popular cultural texts, such as produced by Disney, children are positioned in relation to race, class, and gender. Artifacts come laden with meaning, and yet, in order to make sense of artifacts and identities, it is important to acknowledge these difficulties.

MEDIATING IDENTITY IN PLACE

In cultural historical activity theory (CHAT), scholars such as Guitiérrez and Stone (2000) describe learning as syncretic and as a series of transformative events that shape identities. In their work, Guitiérrez and Stone use the term *syncretic* to mean "principled and strategic use of a combination of theoretical and methodological tools to examine individual actions, as well as the goals and histories of those actions" (Guitiérrez & Stone, 2000, p. 150). Syncretic literacies represent texts and practices that are brought together in novel ways to reinvent cultural practices by individuals in particular contexts. In this way, contexts, such as classrooms, contain visible and invisible features. Within classrooms, individuals are positioned in multiple intellectual, cultural, historical, artifactual, and spatial pathways, and when these pathways are operationalized through teachers and students, they guide what gets learned. In other words, meaning is not fixed in texts, but rather practices and exchanges are socially and culturally mediated (Bakhtin, 1981). Meaning is therefore constructed through individuals and their contact with practices. In the book, we offer a different spin on mediation by arguing that artifacts establish connections between people and places. Cultural historical activity theory proved helpful in teasing out mediating moments between individuals, the things that they value, and places.

In 2003–2004, 3.8 million students in U.S. public schools had limited English skills (National Center for Education Studies, 2008). These students came from all around the world to find a place and identity in the United States. Many rich, varied studies have been conducted across the United States on how first- and second-generation immigrants forge identities in a new, foreign context. Kris Guitiérrez (2009) conducted research with Hispanic families at home and in communities in California exploring ways in which they create diasporas, third spaces to sediment identities in place. Her work illustrates the power of artifacts and space in forging identity in place. Moll, Amanti, Neff, and Gonzalez (1992) examined home literacy practices of Hispanic families in communities in Arizona and how they are tied up with practices and objects in the home that carry funds of knowledge as currency for family members living outside of their homelands (Moll, Amanti, Neff, & Gonzalez, 1992). Cheryl McLean (2008) conducted research in Georgia and more recently in Newark, New Jersey, documenting the life stories and accompanying texts and artifacts of Caribbean youth and how these stories map onto identity construction in the United States. This construction of space and identities provides a platform from which students can access literate identities, as here there is a reason to write, to articulate from a position from which students feel powerful. Critical literacy is about mobilizing that platform using texts; artifactual critical literacy is about mobilizing that platform through artifacts. Artifacts open up worlds that bring in new identities.

LOOKING AT STUDIES OF PRACTICE

Artifactual critical literacy can open up the opportunity to look at artifacts as situated within threads of power and linked to both local and global spaces. An object can be carried across contexts. It is possible to then create listening spaces that honor the exchange of artifacts and thereby create opportunities for critical literacy activities. In the following sections, we present case studies of artifactual critical literacy in community settings.

A Summer Writing Program

In the summer of 2009, I (Jennifer) conducted a 2-week summer writing project through Community House at Princeton University, which is an organization that provides outreach programs for Princeton and neighboring communities. The project represents what Jeffrey and Troman (2004) call "a compressed ethnography," which they describe as involving "a short period of intense ethnographic research in which researchers inhabit a research site almost permanently for anything from a few days to a month" (p. 538). Jeffrey and Troman talk about how compressed ethnographies allow researchers to live the life of inhabitants but within short, intense periods of time.

The summer program involved middle school students from Princeton, Trenton, and other surrounding communities. I worked closely with teachers and students to document their lived experiences, and they completed a survey about their out-of-school/personal interests, backgrounds, languages spoken, family compositions, and so forth. In addition to making observational notes, I interviewed Yousef, an African American college student who was doing an internship at Princeton University and acted as coordinator of the program, and Cameron, who is an English teacher at Princeton High School who taught much of the unit. There were also 11 African and Caribbean American middle school students (age range 12 to 13 years old) involved in the research project, as well as the director of Community House.

The program began with a family night, where the teaching team described the unit of study to parents, and concluded with a celebration event, both of which infused a community, family literacy aspect to the program. I worked closely with Cameron to devise a unit of study built on critical and artifactual literacy. We began the unit by reading excerpts from Barack Obama's (1995) *Dreams from My Father*, and, as an extension assignment, students created a biographical text of their own story. Based on parent feedback from the evening launch of the program, we focused on writing and composition, only we kept the notion of composition open to the use of multiple modes of expression and representation. Since we offered students a choice in how they presented their biography, most students gravitated to genres in which they felt most comfortable. Some students opted for PowerPoint presentations, others created large-format storybooks on Bristol board, and others focused on an artifact and how it tells their story. Over the 2 weeks, we worked with students to shape their biographies. At the end of the 2 weeks, parents came for a public screening and presentation of biographies by each student.

One of the important components of the research was artifact collection and discussions with students about their biography projects. I interviewed five students who agreed to be videotaped about their projects and their valued artifacts. My study represents an example of artifactual critical literacy at work. The premise of the program is that objects such as family photos, a grandmother's necklace, and even the Lincoln Memorial are artifacts that opened up stories for students in the study. Figure 4.1 is a screenshot of a

WASHINGTON D.C.

This year I went to Washington D.C for a school fieldtrip. We had to be on the buses at five in the morning and we came back home around 10:00 at night. It was very exciting to see the different sites. We were able to see the Korean, Vietnam, World War One and Two memorial. We saw the monument of Thomas Jefferson, Albert Einstein and George Washington, and we also visited many Museums. My favorite was the Lincoln Memorial. This was my second time out of New Jersey and in a different state.

Figure 4.1. The Lincoln Memorial.

segment of Belinda's PowerPoint presentation about her own biography. In the slide, Belinda presents a seminal moment in her life—when she saw the Lincoln Memorial on a school trip to Washington, D.C. To her, the Lincoln Memorial typifies a part of her own heritage, and as she said to me, "It gave me a sense of pride."

The project contained core elements of an artifactual critical literacies approach to understanding texts and language: It was personal and used different modes of expression and representation; it was inclusive and encircled one life with a collective; and it extended to another, important text that reflected more traditional literacies students are expected to acquire. Applying artifactual critical literacy makes literacy more meaningful and grounds it in place and subjectivities.

Every Object Tells a Story

The Ferham Families project, described in Chapter 2, resulted in an exhibition of objects and stories at the Rotherham Acts Centre, together with a website designed by Zahir Rafiq. The team then applied for Knowledge Transfer Opportunities Funding, from the University of Sheffield, which I (Kate) worked at, in order to work with a small group of practitioners to develop a set of learning resources to be used in family learning and museum settings and called "Every Object Tells a Story." Sheffield, the nearest city to Rotherham, was a good place to develop and trial the materials because many areas of the city, such as Burngreave, have multilingual communities with diverse family cultures. Therefore, the pack was trialed with a group of families in a family learning setting in collaboration with Sheffield Family Learning and the

Burngreave Family Learning Campaign. A website (www.everyobjecttellsastory .org.uk) was created as a result of this project, with the learning resources free to download from the site, and a repository of the data set available for researchers to access. A group of educators—Jacqui, Parven, and Mumtaz—tried out the activities with families who wanted to improve their literacy skills in a community context. The families were migrants, and these activities were ways of bridging their experiences back home to their new experiences in Sheffield. The following is a selection of these activities.

My Precious Objects: Discussion Ideas. The discussion ideas below could be used with children or adults. Some adults who have recently experienced trauma might find the first question too painful—we found that Somali families in Sheffield would just save their children. However, students might enjoy starting with that question. Discussion topics to develop conversation among the group are as follows:

- Which three objects would you save from your home if there was a fire? Why? Are these objects different from what other members of your family would choose?
- Where do you keep the objects you value the most? At home? In a certain room? On display or locked away?

The educators found that when they worked with families, both adults and children, having them bring their own special objects to class was a way of creating an equal and open space to talk. Here are directions for carrying out the activity:

- Have the students choose an interesting family object with a story behind it (for example, a photograph, ornament, memento from a vacation or a family event such as a wedding, something that has been passed down through their family).
- Look at objects and pictures of objects brought in by students.
- Ask them to consider whether other members of the family would have chosen different objects.
- Introduce your own special object and ask the group to guess its meaning and why you brought it in.

Here, the educators, Parven and Jacqui, who tried out the activity with families in Sheffield, reflect on how it went:

> Members of the group said they enjoyed the session. Learners invited Jacqui and Parven to attend their cultural events—such as musical

class, wedding party—and to visit their house. Some of them offered to show their marriage video. Some of the learners came wearing traditional jewelry and a belt with a Yemeni knife with a case. Parven explained, "The group shared their traditional culture with us and explained the purpose of the use for every object, for example, the belt with a knife holder which is worn on the waist. This is worn when dancing at a cultural event. One of the ladies brought in a dress, and she said that she could bring a picture of her daughter wearing the dress. This shows everyone's enthusiasm for sharing their views on objects they value from their homes."

Longer activities could emerge from this activity, including creating family museums in classrooms or community contexts. An artifactual critical literacy approach would consider ways in which objects have meaning in different contexts. The narratives connected to the objects could be shared, and a community exhibition made of these objects and their stories could be created, with a link to the history of Yemen and of Somalia, in the context of British colonial history and postcolonial identities. This would make the activities critical and globally connected.

Mumtaz Van-der-Vord, a community teacher in Sheffield, also tried out the activity with a group of women, who were adult learners who had come to learn English as a second language. They brought in the following:

- A digital camera
- A gold ring
- A photo of a mother-in-law carrying her granddaughter
- Ornamental praying beads
- A wedding photograph
- A leather purse

Mumtaz then invited each student to tell the story behind her object, and through this process, hidden "ruling passions" were discovered. Mumtaz wrote of the students:

We discovered that Shireen (Malaysian) is a keen photographer; she grew to be interested in photography through sharing her husband's passion in the subject. Shanaz (Pakistani) explained that the engraving on the ring contained the initials of her nieces and nephews and that she longed for a child of her own and when she was to be blessed with one then its initials would also be engraved. Andrea (Polish) brought in a photo of her mother-in-law carrying Andrea's daughter; it was the closest thing she had to her own mother who died before her granddaughter was born. Myra (Egyptian) brought in some praying beads that had been a gift from her old medical school teacher who had also been a mentor to her. Sara (Pakistani) brought in a photo of her wedding day as it represented a time when she was back in her homeland and also represented the start of a journey to a new country. Almas (Malaysian) brought in a purse which was given to her by her best friend back in Malaysia just before Almas left for the UK. (Van-der-Vord, 2008, p. 59)

The experience enabled the group to find out about each other in a much more friendly and accessible way than they had previously. These activities then created opportunities for writing. Telling stories about the objects opened up relationships as well as local and global spaces. In Chapter 7 we expand on this methodology as a way of creating a framework for artifactual critical literacies. By interrogating artifacts in the same way as texts have been interrogated, and then looking at artifacts in relation to their capacity to effect change and a shift in identity and practice, the potential is there within teaching and learning for a more radical space for learning.

Family Memory Books. In a family learning context, families shared object stories. In this activity, the goals for the project included the following:

- Consider the different meanings that objects can have and why some objects have a special value and meaning to individuals
- Discuss as a family which objects in the home mean the most, and compare this with the responses from other families
- Identify and celebrate the special things in the home, and explore how these objects relate to family memories and stories
- Consider the secret stories that objects can hold and the different meaning they have for different people
- Think about the special meaning objects have over time, and find out about how museums take care of and display some of these objects

Families can construct a "family memory book" from loose pages joined together, or by adding items to a purchased scrapbook. Items to add/things to do could include the following:

- A family tree
- Photographs or drawings of family members
- Handprints/footprints

- Drawings and photographs of the objects that are important to the family
- Drawings of other items that reflect family members' interests or passions
- Notes from oral history interviews
- A design for the front cover of the book

The idea of a family book can also be used with multilingual groups and can be a form of storytelling. Artifacts can be points of connection and ways of creating discussion opportunities for groups. These books and collections of artifacts can then be shared within and across communities.

Art, Identity, and Power

Artifacts can be instruments that can lever power. Artifacts can transform identities. Here Zahir Rafiq, who was part of the Ferham Families project described in Chapter 2, talks about how he has developed a positive approach to his work as an Islamic artist in a Western context:

> At the beginning I found it difficult to get into galleries and find spaces for my work to be shown. The major thing for me was having my first exhibition of contemporary Islamic art in a church and this provided a new vision and context for the art work. It was also very important for me in that it had a role in educating people about Islamic faith—and with 9/11 that had more significance and for me it was about really putting yourself out there and really sending positive messages when it was needed. I also created a multi-faith calendar for the South Yorkshire police force. What I want to do is to focus on the contemporary side, to look at British Asian families as a contemporary Islamic artist. I want to explore what is happening with Western art and mix that with Islamic art, and using mosques and textual work but in contemporary ways so that the younger generation can relate to that. (Pahl, Pollard, & Rafiq, 2009, p. 91)

Zahir uses art in a way to effect social change. His work on the Ferham Families project, in displaying artifacts from British Asian families and developing them into a website and museum exhibition, was part of this. As he explains: "If it wasn't for projects like Ferham Families, that kind of thing wouldn't happen and be part of public art work. It has given me lots of opportunities to show my other skills as a designer" (p. 91).

Artists like Zahir who interrogate power relations through art and artifacts can draw on work in critical literacy to create new representations of identity, those that can move forward in inclusive ways to honor new identities. This work can then be moved into critical literacy education. For example, a further step would then be to interrogate the artifacts from the point of view of the following:

- Value: Does value matter in the case of this artifact? If not, why not?
- Timescale: What is the timescale of the artifact? Is it intergenerational?
- Space: What spaces has the artifact inhabited, and how has it traveled?
- Production: Is the artifact found or newly made? How was it made?
- Mode: What modality is most salient and why?
- Relation to institutions of power: Who controls the artifact and its attendant communities?

These categories are discussed in more detail in Chapter 7. They offer the beginnings of a discussion about the critical aspects of artifactual literacy. Discussions, such as the insight that Valerie offered in the opening vignette to this chapter, offer a new hierarchy of artifacts, based on meaning, not commercial value. Students could be encouraged to discuss artifacts in relation to experiences of migration, and new ways of looking at identities can be brought in. These discussions can be recorded, and then students could write their own artifact stories in relation to these different kinds of discussions. The key with artifactual critical literacy is to ask questions of different kinds of objects that then offer students space to tell their stories.

PRIVILEGING THE ARTIFACTUAL

What happens if artifacts are united with a critical literacies perspective? Critical literacies is about accounting for power. Power resides within texts, but it can also be discussed and accounted for during the making of texts and in the uniting of perspectives to collectively create social change. It accounts for different ways of conceptualizing identities, communities, and texts. Critical literacy education is also in-place. It means accounting for communities. By walking through a community, looking at visual signs and experiencing a community fully, a deeper engagement with space and place emerges. Within these spaces are artifacts, embedded in public and private spaces. As we have seen, artifacts let in new kinds of identities and create listening opportunities for communities. Analyzing what students write about when they describe their special artifacts, as the students do in Chapter 5, opens up windows to recognizing and honoring identities. It is then possible to question established hierarchies. Therefore, bringing in artifacts can help harness the questioning implied in critical literacies.

SUMMING UP: ARTIFACTUAL CRITICAL LITERACIES

Artifacts position learners differently. Artifacts open up modalities and sub-jectivities. In this chapter, we argued that there is a complementarity between artifactual literacy and critical literacy because they both strive to empower learners. In the next two chapters, we feature studies that use artifacts as ways of repositioning students in classrooms. Moving from private, lived spaces to the public domains of schooling, artifacts gave participants in the studies a place in schooling and moved them into content-area literacy.

· CHAPTER 5 ·

Adolescent Writing and Artifactual Literacies

If you'd have seen us marching back to those tables with Nemo held over our heads as though we had fought him from the ocean; if you had seen the look on Debbie's face, you'd have been pretty impressed. Even though a lot of people would say we "failed" or "cheated," it makes me proud to think back to those days of unbridled determination to give someone a small but significant gift. Debbie had a lot of different kinds of cancer, and she's gone now. We put Nemo, along with some other things that had a funny story attached, in her casket. It made us a little less sad to remember all the great adventures we'd been on and the hilarious circumstances we'd found ourselves in. I know I won't forget that trip to Morey's Piers or that Nemo plushie and how we all worked so hard to get him. Maybe you, the reader, thinks it's stupid, or insignificant, but it makes me proud. . . . I wonder if the lady at the duck game still remembers me.

—Sienna, age 14

IN THIS CHAPTER, we focus on artifactual literacies as an approach into writing. We look at a particular population of ninth-grade students and how their artifactual worlds open up a space for writing. Carried over from previous chapters, there is an acknowledgment that artifacts shore up identities in contexts, allowing individuals to find a place where they did not have one before. Artifacts can be a bridge into different writing genres. Biographical, persuasive, historical, and personal writing—even the beloved five-paragraph essay—can all be taught through the prism of valued objects. This chapter extends our account of artifacts, neighborhoods, talk, and critical literacy by looking at a research study in which I (Jennifer) was engaged (see Appendix A). This study looked at student artifacts and their figured worlds (Holland et al., 1998) in conjunction with the particular setting of their school.

73

The multiyear study took place in Princeton, New Jersey, with 20 to 30 ninth-grade students each year taking an English support class. Students in this class had done poorly on the Grade Eight Proficiency Assessment Test (GEPA). Students in the support English class were not obliged to be part of the research study, but all of the students with one exception agreed to participate. To conduct the research, I sought out four experienced, talented teachers to work with me as a team—we met regularly, kept journals, took entry and exit surveys, and interviewed each student about his or her choice of artifacts. A key member of the team was Jackie Delaware, a gifted teacher who really cares about her students. Jackie is committed to helping struggling students appreciate English literature.

The narrative in the chapter opening about a stuffed Nemo, which is a fish in the Disney film *Finding Nemo*, was written by a student participant, Sienna, as an ode to a special object in response to the topic "An Artifact That Recalls a Memory." Sienna is 14 years old, shy and unassuming, with a deft attention to detail in her writing, especially when it comes to objects and moments that matter to her. What makes the reflection so vivid is Sienna's clear picture not only of a remembered moment but also of how an object embodies that moment. Through a simple phrase, without syrupy emotion, but in a matter-of-fact way, Sienna tells us about Debbie, a friend she lost to cancer. As a writer, Sienna tempers melancholy with levity, and she uses form to shape content—separating the brief but fitting conclusion, "I wonder if the lady at the duck game still remembers me," to signal what the event meant to her. There is no doubt that Sienna is a writer, yet she does not excel in English, and for this reason, she was part of the support English class. She is one of seven student writers showcased in this chapter.

THE COMMUNITY AND UNDERACHIEVEMENT

Princeton is a university town equidistant from New York and Philadelphia. It is a town where great writers like Toni Morrison live and great minds flock to discuss such issues as the flagging economy and ways of unifying Iraq. It is predominately White, middle class, and suburban—not the first place that one would think of when researching a setting about a lack of motivation in English teaching and learning. One of the more interesting aspects of Princeton is the Clay Street area in the center of town, which is home to a long-standing African and Caribbean American community and a burgeoning Latino population from Guatemala, Mexico, and Peru.

Princeton High School mirrors the values of the community with its emphasis on academic and cultural achievement. Yet in the fall of 2004, the high school did not make adequate yearly progress (AYP), and there is a growing population of students who are not doing well in a variety of subject areas, especially in English.

At Princeton High School, as with any school subject to state pre-specified objectives and expectations, literacy learning in secondary school focuses on reading and writing formal paper-based texts, often canonical texts, using predetermined rules surrounding the understanding of English. This view sees literacy as an autonomous, value-free attribute that any individual can master with time and determination and that can be measured and tested by standardized tests of literacy competence, such as the GEPA in New Jersey. By "autonomous," we mean the perspective, often favored by governments focused on a skills agenda, that sees literacy as a universal, reified view of skills development, as opposed to an "ideological" model, which views literacy as part of human experiences that shifts based on contexts (Street, 1984).

Labeled as "underachieving" in literacy, students in the support English class received a low GEPA and were identified by English teachers as requiring extra support. At school, many of the participants involved in the study exist within an autonomous model wherein literacy competence is evaluated through standardized measures such as summative assessments like the GEPA, but also within a more ideological model wherein teachers build on students' knowledge and experiences to inform teaching.

The school district description of this support English class states that the course objective is fostering "reading comprehension, vocabulary development, writing skills, homework, and research projects." The purpose of the ninth-grade course is to help students achieve by providing "opportunities for supervised completion of their assignments, assistance with skills development, and motivational activities to inspire commitment to English learning." Essential questions to the course are:

- How does reading enrich a life?
- How can a learner build on prior knowledge, reflection, and determination to achieve success?
- How does the setting of goals lead to success?
- Why is it crucial to understand not only what we learn, but how we learn?

Many of these goals are laudable and would certainly help the students, who are indeed "underachieving" in literacy, with English reading and writing.

What these students do well is invest in artifacts and actions that interest them and, what is more, etch that commitment in their written narratives.

From the beginning of the research, the research team opted to situate English teaching within the artifactual and material worlds of teenagers. A surprising element of the research for me was how wide-ranging and diverse interests and associated texts were for the students. With a group of ninth-grade students, it is expected that they would talk about cell phones, video games, and Facebook, but instead, one wrote about a necklace from her grandmother; another, about running shoes he wears to wrestle; and Sienna, about a Nemo plushie that evokes a memory. Not only are these artifacts eclectic, but the written narratives about them are wrought with detail, emotion, even wisdom.

TRAVELING ARTIFACTS THAT RECONFIGURE IDENTITY

With the concept of valued artifacts as a bridge into written narratives in mind, this chapter views artifacts as a means to reconfigure students who feel marginalized by school literacy to find a place in the English classroom. Literate practices are seen through artifacts that can be regarded as *artifacts of identity* (Holland et al., 1998). Artifacts of identity resurrect what Holland and colleagues describe as "figured worlds," which are "contexts of meaning for actions, cultural production, performances, disputes, for the understandings that people come to make of themselves, and for the capabilities that people develop to direct their own behavior in these worlds" (p. 6). The teenagers described in this chapter drew on their figured worlds to situate themselves in English class. What is central to our argument in this book is that artifacts open up figured worlds. When artifacts travel across contexts, they can and do reconfigure identity. Artifacts leverage power for students. A bracelet, wrestling shoes, a Nemo plushie imbue power and relevance into learning and serve as a motivating catalyst to writing.

Artifacts often carry with them what Lemke (2000) describes as "timescales." For example, a wallet that you have had since you were young, given to you by someone who is part of your life story, carries a longer timescale than a textbook that you used in ninth-grade English class. Lemke has argued that the semiotic potential of an artifact is linked to its timescale. For example, a Samurai sword carries longer and deeper meaning potential than an ordinary household knife due to its deeper and richer timescale.

Artifacts produced by people, such as drawings or sculptures, can be seen as a process by which identities are sedimented into texts (Rowsell & Pahl, 2007). A child may watch her mother draw kitchen plans. She might also learn to draw a map at school. As she learns about the social practice of making plans, she creates a new text, a plan of her house that includes a box of candy. Within this plan, aspects of a child's identity (e.g., a love of sweets) are discerned sedimented within the plan (Pahl, 2007a). Holland

and Leander (2004) theorize a similar notion that they call "laminated identity" in texts. Artifactual narratives featured later in the chapter can be seen as produced through complex interpersonal relations. They carry within them traces of their making, and because many of the artifacts were collaborative and interpersonal, identities can be seen laminated within these material objects.

Thinking and writing about valued artifacts enact parts of identities. By *enact*, we mean how valued artifacts constitute and manage identities. This chapter presents a study that resituates marginalized students back into school space. The chapter sets out a heuristic enabling us to see the power of everyday artifacts in a new light. A range of identities are presented in the case studies that follow; these case studies are by no means exhaustive, but rather a sample of practices that artifacts can invoke and practices that can be used to make meaning in literacy classrooms.

Balancing traditional literacy with traveling artifacts meant that student identities were reconfigured. In this way, literacy is seen as complex and semiotically framed within a competency model of literacy acquisition. Literacy practices grow out of an understanding of contexts. By having valued artifacts travel into schooling, whereby students are able to draw on the semiotic resources of these artifacts, literacy becomes relevant to student participants.

The students in the support English class do not need extra support in English—they need reasons why English is relevant to them and to their lives. Student participants consistently expressed—in writing, class discussions, and interviews—their strong ties to family and to their community as a source of inspiration. These students often work after school, care for siblings, and, in general, take on family welfare as a part of their everyday lives. Table 5.1 describes some of the students, providing background information and particular literacy struggles based on interviews, and their valued artifacts. Maynor, Jasmin, and Sienna, to name a few students, need to know that their worlds are not that far removed from Odysseus and Othello and, perhaps most important, that teachers value their experiences.

MEDIATING THE "LIFE-WORLDS" OF YOUNG PEOPLE WITH LITERARY WORLDS

The teachers and I designed the research study in the English support class to mediate the "life-worlds" of young people with the literary worlds of the required course texts. In each of the first 2 years of the research project, student participants wrote six narratives about valued objects. In May, students presented their written narratives in a portfolio, which they designed.

Table 5.1. Student participation profiles.

Student	Background Information (Age, Race, Culture)	Struggle with Literacy	Ethnographic/ Local Standpoint	Artifacts of Interest
1. Sienna (2nd year)	14, White, Native American, and Irish	Feels like she procrastinates with assignments and has difficulty organizing herself for school	Frequents community center for skating and has developed keen interest in manga from neighbor	Drawing of female manga warrior
2. Rob (2nd year)	14, White, Russian, and Jewish	Feels "moderate" about school texts	Has a keen interest in news and the stock exchange: writes stories in his spare time	An ode to an Internet rooter
3. John (2nd year)	14, White, American, and Jewish	Lacks interest in books for English class	Is an avid sports player and is keen on Madden football video game; has a passion for cooking	Guitar Hero
4. Jasmin (2nd year)	15, African American	Does not feel a connection with books studied in English class	Has a part-time job in the community and likes to text friends	History of hip-hop and a video of her dancing
5. Liam (2nd year)	14, Venezualan American and Irish	Finds it hard to get motivated to finish work in English class	Plays Airsoft in local parks with friends	Narrative about blanky
6. Lila (1st and 2nd years)	14, Guatemalan and Mexican	Likes writing per-suasive and personal essays but does not enjoy more formal essay writing	Likes to write in her journal and talk to her friends	Friendship bracelet
7. Maynor (2nd year)	14, Mexican	Does not have confidence in his writing	Likes to write in his journal and to write stories	Picture of sunset and paper crane
8. Winston (2nd year)	14, Haitian American	Is not interested in traditional texts	Likes to skateboard around Princeton with friends	Photo gallery
9. Calvin (2nd year)	14, African American	Does not like many of the books that he studies in English class and is not keen on writing	Likes video games and football	A wallet and a memory
10. Mark (2nd year)	14, White, American	Does not like to write essays; is more of an artist	Likes to wrestle and sculpt	His running shoes

There was a community event at the end of the schoolyear to which members of the community came to hear students present their artifactual portfolios. In the third year, Jackie and I revised the course to include a digital component. In the fall semester, students created digital stories based on Homer's *The Odyssey* (1996), as presented in Chapter 6; in the spring semester, students created Facebook pages in a Word document format on characters in Richard Wright's *Black Boy* (1945). What became clear from the beginning was that the student participants value the artifacts in their lives over many of the texts studied in English class, which bear little relation to their own worlds.

Literature as artifactual helps students tie artifactual dimensions of character worlds in canonical texts to their own individual, artifactual worlds. By harnessing canonical texts to digital and multimodal assignments such as Facebook, students build on their tacit understanding and appreciation of multimodal texts within more traditional, written texts. For example, in creating Facebook profiles for characters in *Black Boy*, such as Richard or Bessie, students drew on their digital practices to do a Google search on popular music in the 1920s and then speculated on the kinds of music, literature, and interests that the novel's characters would enjoy.

The assignment compels students to think about what characters value and why, who is in their inner circle, and how to multimodally represent the characters. To create a Facebook profile, students had to choose a photo that resembled the description of the character, create a typical dialogue that the character might have on his or her Wall, and even choose particular games or applications that the character might use. Figure 5.1 shows a student-designed Facebook page for Bessie from *Black Boy*.

As in many schools, there are security filters on the Princeton High School computers, preventing students from accessing websites such as Facebook or YouTube. To re-create a Facebook-feel without actually using it, Jackie and Jamie (a student teacher) devised a Facebook template in Microsoft Word. The template did not have a social networking device; however, it allowed students to design profile pages, insert photographs, add Wall comments, and broadly inhabit the characters in Wright's novel through a familiar participatory structure. Creating a Facebook page compels students to inhabit the characters' worlds: speculate on their turns of phrase, prefer one visual over another, choose a favorite song and saying that fits their character. Even students who did not like or did not have access to Facebook were familiar with the practices of social networking.

A common characteristic among the student participants was an inability to understand what Brian Street (2009) describes as "academic literacies." As one of the teachers on the team said, "The difference between these students and the A students is that they do not know how to *do* school." As

Facebook Forum

Name of character: Bess<3
Birthday: March 25, 1908
Sex: Female
Marital Status: Single ;)
Current Location: Memphis
Political Views: none

Personal Info:

Email address: iwantlove@aol.com

AIM Screen name: singlelady17

Activities: Look for people to make mine!!!

Favorite Music: "The Desert Song"

Favorite Books: <u>Little Book of Fairy Stories</u>

Favorite Quote: "treat me like an angel and ill take you to heaven"

Groups: Meet your perfect match; online speed dating

Figure 5.1. Bessie and her Facebook page.

already pointed out, there is a hidden demographic of students at Princeton High School who do not have the explicit framing of discourses and practices of A students—for example, how to shift registers and discourse from an English paper on *The Odyssey* to a paper on the American Civil War. An explicit, tacit switch in register requires an understanding of academic literacies. One of the hallmarks of an A student is the ability to adhere to academic conventions that accomplish desired rhetorical and aesthetic effects in writing. By using objects as a vehicle into writing voices and materializing almost artifactual qualities to written narratives, we sought to enable students to develop an understanding of and appreciation for academic literacies.

TRAVELING OBJECTS AND RECONFIGURED IDENTITIES

Different facets of artifactual literacy as an approach are illustrated by the writing samples presented in this section, which are quoted verbatim to present an authentic picture of the students' meaning making. Each student chooses a mode and medium to best suit his or her message. The assignment that the teachers gave students was to write reflections about valued artifacts with certain topics in mind, such as friendship, success, family, and so forth.

Artifacts have cultural biographies—that is, artifacts accumulate histories, and these histories reflect back on those who value the objects. Tracing the biography of an artifact, and linking it to the biography of a person, reconfigures identities. The centrality of artifacts to the students was clear from the fluency of their writing, but artifacts signaled different sorts of practices and ideologies for each participant. What is more, over time the meaning of artifacts shifted. Artifacts can create tensions for identities, and they can be put to work to manage those tensions. The first artifactual writing below gives a glimpse into a family narrative. Analyzing written reflections about artifacts gives us a window into what participants think about and what absorbs their time. Uncovering a dynamic interplay of the biography of artifacts with identity practices helps us to make a connection to another context.

Maynor and His Sunset

Maynor was born in Mexico and soon afterward moved to Princeton, New Jersey. At 14, Maynor is shy and describes himself as "quiet, smart, and heavy." When speaking with Maynor about his cooking or other interests, he becomes alive and animated. His writing is both eloquent and explicit. After his first reflection, it became apparent that he *is* a writer.

The Sunset

The artifact I chose was something my mom gave to me. The artifact is a picture of the sun setting in the horizon in a vast ocean, the sun is halfway on the horizon and the sea reflects its image for miles. The sun itself looks like an orb of gold, and the suns rays makes the sky turn from purple to red to orange and to yellow, while the clouds are wide and they radiate with the glow from the sun, making them a golden orange. Then the sea is a dark blue with a wave of light upon it which shows the reflection of the sun, and the waves are small but visible enough to see.

This artifact was given to my mom because she really liked it when she saw it and thought that I would like it, and of course I did. It is special to me because a sunset in real time sets for about 30 to 60 minutes while a picture of a sunset lasts forever and it captures the beauty of the sun.

If I never met my Mom, I would never have received the poster of the sunset, and she is important to me because she is the only one who will love me no matter what and I have known her my whole life. And she has taught me that the smallest things are the ones we take for granted. I chose this because it means a lot to me because it was a gift from the heart, and if I ever lost it, it would be like if a piece of me was taken. (May 9, 2008)

There is so much in Maynor's reflection. Upon first reading it, Maynor's writing sounds so explicit and vivid, with such details as "a sunset in real time" interspersed with authentic feelings such as "if I ever lost it, it would be like a piece of me was taken." Maynor captures detail so well; like Sienna, he is specific about what he sees. He is able to blend details with facts. We come to know things about Maynor in reading his narrative: He is close to his mom, he is visually acute, and he values objects in his life. He does not take for granted talismans around him that betoken parts of his figured worlds. What was obvious to me as a researcher is that Maynor made a connection between his valued objects crossing into English class, and he writes eloquently about this connection.

Jasmin and Hip-Hop

A 14-year-old, Jasmin is African American with bright eyes, lots of energy, and a strong attachment to friends. Jasmin is a dancer and loved the idea of incorporating her dancing into English class. For one of her artifacts, Jasmin created a dance video with a scripted voice-over, provided below:

Script Accompanying Dance Video of Jasmin Dancing Hip-Hop

Hip Hop dancing began in the early 70's it started out with reggae dancing. It was brought to us through New York and Brookland. It was naturally an African American type dance that started out with people beat boxing with their mouths. Hip Hop dancing started out mainly with break dancing which many Hip Hoppers call the old school, and escalated more and more into what Hip Hop looks like today which kids call the new school. Hip Hop is mainly known for its street style look. Unlike jazz or ballet Hip Hop is more loose and easier because you are more capable of adding in your own "flava." The word Hip Hop was given to us by multiple Djs who used them when they were beat boxing. It was Dj Afrika Bambaataa who made the words clear to us and it is the reason why we all use the term Hip Hop. Hip Hop started a lot of the dances done today like tap dancing and the salsa, which started out as a dance done in the up-right position which we called "top rockin" back in the day. Certain styles of the Hip Hop dance came from martial arts movies that came out back in the 70's which were put to the beat of Hip Hop music. The first spin ever done in Hip Hop was "pencils" which is a full spin done on the head. Ken Swift Hip Hoppers made the laws of physics useful when they did hip Hip Hop especially when they did their "pencils". The form of "locking" was originated by Don Campbell, also known as Don Camellock when he was trying to imitate a dance called "the funky chicken". That is when the group the electronic boogaloo lockers were formed they were the best dancers known in 1976, they put all the forms of hip hop together and everybody loved them and they were known as the best hip hoppers ever. Today, Hip Hop dance is mostly used for competition. It is still fun to African Americans but spread very quickly to other races as well. Hip Hop is the finest type of dance around. Unlike back in the day though hip hop isn't used for beat boxing and barely has any break dancing in it but is still clearly a very popular type of dance and as time goes on I hope it stays that way.

As with Maynor's writing, Jasmin's script is filled with details and distinctive turns of phrase. In her voice-over, it is obvious that Jasmin has researched the history of hip-hop and taken the task on with zeal. Rhetorically, she emulates a historical, documentary voice with phrases like "back in the day." Jasmin imbued a particular voice into her voice-over using words such as "flava" and "top rockin" to mirror tone with content. In this way, Jasmin exhibits an understanding of register, of discourse, of linguistic tropes in another genre, which she emulates in both the form and content of her artifact reflection. The movement that accompanies her voice-over is another form of expression of her passion for hip-hop; to add to the expressiveness, her dad tape-recorded her dance sequence and she edited the voice-over to time it perfectly with each move.

Lila and Her Friendship Bracelet

Lila was 14 when I met her. Her mother is from Guatemala, and her father is from Mexico. When I asked her what she likes to do outside of school, Lila said, "I like to write about what I am feeling and I like to write songs." At one moment in our interview, Lila talked about contrasts in cultural assumptions and practices in Hispanic cultures versus White American/European practices:

> Well, my Mom is Hispanic and she was not used to the idea of seeing her child go and stay over night at a friend's houses. It took my Mom a while to understand it and it's like she had to adapt to some more American ways and when it comes to situations like that is when I think about being Hispanic and American. (February 5, 2008)

Lila sits between worlds of cultural practices at home and American practices, a fact that emerges in her writing. Lila values her friendships, and two of her written narratives were about valued objects that a friend gave her. Friends are clearly a bridge to her American identity. The narrative below recounts the origins of a friendship bracelet that she wears:

> The artifact I've chosen to represent not only loyalty but also true friendship is my very own friendship bracelet. My friendship bracelet was given to me by one of my best friend. Her name is Dorothy. The bracelet is light blue, my favorite color and it has three rhinestonces D, L, M and a heart. The letters stand for Dorothy, Lila, and Maria, it represents how special we are to one another and that no matter what we will be there for each other. Dorothy and Maria each have a friendship bracelet as well each in their own favorite color. I remember it was two years ago when Dorothy, Maria and I decided to get a friendship bracelet; we each received it on our birthdays. The reason why we got the bracelet in the first place was to remind us we were always together no matter what. I remember when we were growing up we all went to different schools so it was hard for us to see each other every day. We hung out during the weekends and occasionally during spring and winter break. Even though school and after school activities kept us apart, we always seemed to end up together and that is how everyone saw us, together. . . . The friendship bracelet is just something we like to have with us when we have our most vulnerable moments. This is why my friendship bracelet is the artifact I chose to represent loyalty and true friendship. (June 11, 2008)

When reading Lila's narrative, what comes out strongly is how her friends anchored her American identity. Through her early friendships in elementary school, Lila found a place in the United States. The bracelet serves as a reminder of her connection to her community.

Calvin and His Grandma

Calvin is 14, tall, Caribbean American, and likes to kid around with Winston. The first time I met Calvin he was joking around in the hallway with his friends. Calvin is lighthearted, funny, at times irreverent, but that is part of his charm. As with all the participants, Calvin took a different tone when he sat and chatted with me. That is, he became far more introspective. It was so clear to me that Calvin wanted to do well in school for himself and for his family. It is with this background knowledge about Calvin that I read his preface to an artifact reflection about a wallet that his grandmother gave to him. The prelude to the artifact reflection recalls the moment his grandmother became ill and went to hospital.

> Oh, the ride home. My grandmother was in the hospital, because of her hart, every day I would go visit her but yesterday my aunt left me before I could go with her to visit my grandmother at the hospital. All day in school I was looking forward to seeing her, my grandma is the best person in the world, now in hospital. She was all ways there for me the person I would go to, to talk to for wisdom to give me an answer. As I gazed out the window of my school bus watching the trees sip by, then my house is close so the bus slows down, I am home. As I stand up in the bus isle and look down it seems to go on for miles, I began to walk I finally made it to the front step. I cross the street and slowly enter my house. Full of excitement and now anxious to find the closest person with a license to take me to the hospital. I rushed to find my Mom but when I found her she had a very worried look on her face and I immediately knew something was wrong I was hoping it had nothing to do with my grandmother.
> "Mom, what's wrong?" I said
> She replies. "it's your grandma she, she's in a better place now."
> I couldn't believe this my heart sunk my eyes filled with tears and I began to cry and could not stop. I cried so hard I could not breath. Why must she die today. 13 years of my life I spent with her, hearing her voice and smelling her scent. When I was sick or upset she would comfort me. I wish I could went with my aunt to see her in her last hours of her life on earth. (June 4, 2008)

Calvin goes on to describe the wallet his grandmother gave him. It is a brown leather wallet with "Indian carvings, pictures of canoes, trees, and bears." Calvin went into great detail about "an eagle that looks amazing and elegant and holding an olive branch in one talon and arrows in the other." Calvin describes the olive branch as a symbol of peace. When Calvin's grandma gave him the wallet, she said, "Calvin, I am going to give you this wallet and promise me you will do good in your life and don't mess it up and make something of yourself." Clearly that phrase made a strong impression on Calvin.

Winston's Photo Gallery

Also 14 years old, Winston is Caribbean American, athletic, loves the Phillies, and, like Calvin, enjoys goofing around with friends. From the outset,

Winston seemed reticent about the artifact project, but in the end, he exhibited great pride in the final product. Winston decided to talk about a series of photographs of his community. Favored places and images were showcased in his PowerPoint presentation. Figure 5.2 shows four of the photographs that Winston presented as visual artifacts of his community.

Winston opted for an oral account of photographs over a written narrative. He presented his photographs to the principal of Princeton High School and a group of peers at the celebration event at the end of the schoolyear. There is a shadow of Winston in the photographs, to reflect his presence in the community. Winston chose photographs as his preferred mode of expression because it reminded him of Facebook and presenting parts of his life to friends.

Sienna and Anime

Sienna's artifactually based writing began this chapter. Sienna is 15, White, Anglo-Saxon with some Native Indian heritage, and describes herself as creative, funny, talkative, and articulate. The first time I met her, we immediately

Figure 5.2. Winston's photo collage.

felt comfortable with each other, and she shared some of her many anime illustrations with me.

During our many conversations, Sienna discussed her passion for manga and anime. Sienna talked about her struggles with literacy, which she attributes to procrastinating with homework due to a lack of interest. Sienna spends most of her time reading manga and anime and creating her own characters. One day in class, she drew the anime warrior shown in Figure 5.3. Sienna loves anime because "characters are not good and evil as they are in books that we study in English, they are in-between, sometimes good and sometimes bad." The illustration shows a female warrior with ribbons covering parts of her body. The character is mostly good, but she has a dark side that comes out sometimes. Sienna claims that, "I relate to anime far more because I appreciate that there are dark sides to people and that becomes a part of my stories and my pictures." Sienna exhibits

Figure 5.3. Sienna's anime figure.

an understanding of story and character development as well as definitive interests in different genres of texts.

Rob and the Internet Rooter

A 14-year-old, Russian, Jewish teenager who has wide-ranging interests in video games from Halo 2 to Paintball, Rob talked about his Internet rooter as an expression of his passion for digital technologies.

> One object that represents a struggle that I am currently facing is my wireless Internet rooter. For me, the Internet is a huge distraction from my school work and can keep me off task for long periods of time. My parents realized and set verbal Internet restrictions. I obviously do not listen. The next thing was putting software on the computer to restrict certain websites; this was easily bypassed with the use of proxies. Next was a boot password (a password set that must be typed in before the computer would start). This was a challenge but after minimal research my brother and I found out we could disable this by removing a pin from the motherboard. So, finally my Dad took our computer away all together. This was the most effective but eventually we found them and simply restored this to their rightful owners, us. Finally my father bought a wireless router with built-in software restricting the access to whatever my father set. This is when my brother and I bought our own routers. (June 11, 2008)

I did not come to know Rob as well as the other students because he was very quiet during class. In an interview, Robert spoke with me about his love of video games and regular viewing of Lost and Prison Break. His artifact reflection revealed his sense of humor and a capacity to imbue a voice into writing (e.g., "I obviously do not listen."). Rob's detailed description of the father–son antics with computer access is both witty and exacting. There is a level of detail that clearly displays his keen interest in the topic.

What the samples above illustrate is that these students *are* writers. They can weave in rhetorical devices, invoke images, and even use literary devices such as parallelism. Yet another discovery is that beyond their cool, nonchalant demeanors lies a strong attachment to their family, friends, and community. Artifacts allowed us to appreciate these features of adolescent meaning making. A text, any text, holds social worlds—the social worlds in which it is made and the ones in which the text is made meaningful. Student narratives about valued objects are texts that encapsulate cultural truth *as it is seen by the writer* and that show how artifactual literacies can be an enabling and powerful way into writing.

RECONFIGURED IDENTITIES THROUGH ARTIFACTUAL LITERACIES

A language and way of approaching and thinking anew about modern writing practices emerge from these case studies. Each piece of writing demonstrates a particular gift, a competence the writer carries with him or her. Maynor has honed the delicate art of expressive language. Jasmin's love of hip-hop led to a historical discourse in her narrative and a keen interest in the genesis of her favorite genre of music. Lila used rhetorical devices in her writing to express what her friendships have meant to her. Calvin, a reluctant writer, re-created a moment in time with exactly the right amount of pathos for a reader to understand the impact of his grandmother's passing. Sienna has such a writer's voice that it is a wonder that she would be considered a struggling literacy learner. Winston can tell a story to anyone and has such strong visual literacy and capacity to capture a mood in a photograph. Rob infuses humor into his writing and is able to be self-reflective enough to embed his own perspective in his writing. All of these skills are valuable as a literate person. They exhibit an appreciation of discourse, of genre switches, of the affordances of modalities, of register, of imbuing ideologies into prose. Table 5.2 showcases each participant, their heuristic as displayed in

Table 5.2. Student participants and their pathway into meaning-making.

Participant	Thinking Frames	Implied Practice
Maynor	Interpersonal artifacts and timescale artifact	Able to recognize the symbolic nature of objects that are dialogic and can ventriloquate relationships
		Able to express how objects betoken people, figured worlds, and histories
Jasmin	Mimetic artifacts/ simulates media	Able to take on a discourse and use the rhetoric effectively
Lila	Signifying artifact	Able to recognize artifacts as indicative of something or signifying people
Calvin	Artifacts of a moment	Able to describe a moment through an artifact
Sienna	Intertextual artifact	Able to describe intertextuality within an artifact
Winston	Artifact as aesthetic expression	Able to use affordance of mode for expression
Rob	Artifact of identity	Able to relate artifact to subjectivities

their written narratives, and implied practices. Admittedly, there are spelling and punctuation mistakes in the writing samples, but there are plenty of literary skills on prominent display. Mechanics, spelling, and syntax were addressed as a part of the editorial process; by extending their material worlds, we could work with students more on their language skills and, eventually, reconfigure their identities *in* school so that they came to derive the same excitement from five-paragraph essays. None of these skills exhibit a struggle with English learning and certainly belie a need for support.

If it is not obvious yet, students showcased in this chapter are often bored in school. It is too easy to blame their teachers, and, actually, their teachers are very good. Over the course of the research, I have developed such respect for the complexity of teenage worlds and the meaning and potential that they hold. What this growing population of students needs is a pedagogy and teaching that speaks to their multimodal sensibilities and their artifactual worlds. There are two important points here: (1) These students can and do express themselves well in a variety of modalities; (2) as educators, we need to listen to and understand student voices.

Every time I go into local hubs close to the high school, like the majestic Princeton Library, I think about students like Sienna and Maynor who made tiles in a large installation hung by the front doors of Princeton Library. The installation, *Happy World*, comprises hundreds of 3-inch-square tiles forged together by the international artist Ik-Joong Kang. *Happy World* reminds me of what Jackie and I have been trying to achieve with student participants, which is to use their material worlds, their everyday, their habitus to open up their field of practice.

As seen in Figure 5.4, Kang joined a series of eclectic tiles as artifacts of the community, the general and the particular fused as an expression of Princeton's diverse domains of practice and cultural stories; Kang deliberately stitched together the individual stories of community members in public artwork. After Princeton Library commissioned a work by Kang, they put advertisements in local newspapers such as *Town Topics* asking community members to contribute meaningful artifacts, or what Holland and colleagues call "artifacts of identity" (Holland et al., 1998). About 1,000 tiles were collected to compose *Happy World*. Kang embedded his own woodcuts on tiles interspersed with community artifacts on tiles. Note that there are disparate objects superimposed on the tiles, such as a football, letters from the old Princeton Library, and two very small globes in a box.

Happy World carries with it such iconic Princeton symbols as Albert Einstein's playing cards set in Plexiglas; a lacrosse stick (the official sport of Princeton); a first-day-of-issue Paul Robeson stamp; catalogue cards from the former library; a bike bell from Kopps, a legendary Princeton

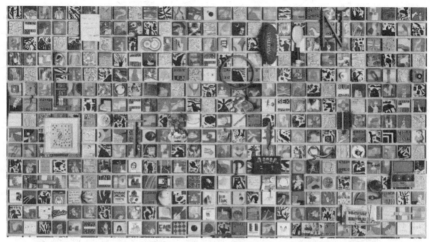

Figure 5.4. Detail from *Happy World*, by Ik-Joong Kang.

bike shop; and Robert Oppenheimer's autograph. Interwoven with Princeton icons were treasured objects such as pieces of concrete from the Berlin Wall; several tiles by children who are bilingual in languages as wide-ranging as Arabic, Urdu, Armenian, Hindi, Estonian, Spanish, French, Turkish, and Georgian, all expressing the diversity present in Princeton. There are photographs of children in the community, a rubber ducky, buttons, a Brownie camera, Spiderman pictures, and endless other memories fossilized in tiles.

Happy World embodies an artifactual approach to meaning making. You could spend an afternoon looking at each and every tile, interpreting its story and its contributor. The library is creating a website where you can click on each tile and hear the story behind the artifact. If only every community could fossilize its members in a colorful installation to celebrate the solace we derive from the things that we love.

SUMMING UP: ADOLESCENT WRITING AND ARTIFACTUAL LITERACIES

To sum up, this chapter has showed how surprising, how colorful, and how expressive artifactual stories are. There is a transformation that occurs when these are brought into writing: The writing speaks of what the writers know but also stretches the limits of their knowing. Many assessment regimes ask for this kind of extension of writing but rein in students' imaginations when it comes to listening to their life-worlds. Literacy through opening up students' lifeworlds looks different. It is a sensory-embodied experience—visual, such as the golden orb of Maynor's sunset; aural, such as the sound of a grandmother's voice or the beat of hip-hop; tactile, as in the feel of a friendship bracelet. These accounts of artifacts evoke the sensory, embodied lived experience of the everyday (Pink, 2009). By accessing this and giving space to it, life is breathed into meaning making.

CHAPTER 6

Digital Storytelling as Artifactual

The sharing of family stories is really wonderful, and is really important for the family. In terms of educational goals, it is the experience of listening, and experience of filming and recording, the process of putting the story together so it makes sense of the experience—that then seeps into a lot of literacy, speaking and listening and that is what we are interested in.

—Class teacher, My Family, My Story

IN THIS CHAPTER, we move to the world of the digital. As the teacher describes above, the sharing of family stories provides a listening opportunity. "The process of putting the story together" creates literacy opportunities, it "seeps into . . . literacy." We have found in our recent projects that digital media can wonderfully evoke the artifactual. While real objects can be present within a space, the creating of a digital story, using sound, photographic images, and moving images, is a powerful way to harness artifactual literacies. Here we describe how that can be done and provide a rationale as well as a detailed account of actual practice. In order to do that, we introduce you to three digital storytellers: Patsy and Manuel, from New Jersey, and Lucy and her family, from North Yorkshire in the United Kingdom. We explore their ruling passions and experience how they found their stories—from bits of their past, from objects in their homes—and how these were crafted and shaped into digital stories. These digital stories were handmade and crafted, just like stories told on paper, with images and words, but they included three-dimensional artifacts that brought them alive to the audiences. Sound, color, texture, shape, and story provided a new repertoire for these meaning makers to tell their stories more fully.

In this chapter we begin with three case studies of digital storytelling and then take up the theoretical underpinning of the approach. Finally, we interrogate the "how," giving a practical account of how digital storytelling can be done in classrooms. As an artifactual literacy, digital storytelling can enable artifacts to come into the classroom in an accessible way, and the relationship between precious objects and stories can be showcased within the digital story. We believe that in this way of working the artifactual can be transformed into story, narrated, and then can itself transform practice, both inside the classroom and in everyday life. Identities are reshaped by hearing stories represented anew.

THREE DIGITAL STORYTELLERS

Digital stories involve a number of different modalities including sound, movement, visuals, color, texture, and the overall material qualities. The level of choice and the interest that the meaning makers put into the modes give them the ability to layer and deeply infuse their texts with multiple meaning. The effect is a dense text. Digital stories are complex narratives by virtue of the multiple modalities that combine in one text. They are multifaceted stories, handmade but also polished and crafted, infused with a personal investment. They are sedimented pieces of habitus. Fractal parts of practice, together with identity, are embedded, shard-like, within the digital story.

The people who made the stories in this chapter—Patsy and Manuel, Lucy and her family—all started the project from the position of being outsiders. They were disconnected from meaning making in schooled contexts. Their family experiences were vivid and real, but within school contexts they remained less visible and, in the case of the high school students, were at risk of school failure. Lucy's children were seen as "quiet" within the classroom, particularly her middle son, and Patsy and Manuel were identified as struggling with English. We found that in accessing the material and in invoking modalities, these individuals were able to sediment an identity that spoke to them and represented something more than the identity visible in the school contexts. Their digital stories bear the traces of a movement from being outside an experience to being inside.

The stories are placed within a context. Street (1993) speaks of how literacy practices can be linked to outside contexts, such as home, workplace, and school, and thereby describes literacy as "ideological." In the same way, multimodal meaning making is linked to context. Therefore, in this chapter, we argue that the meaning makers' choices of modalities are ideologically situated. For example, Patsy, by choosing to represent handmade dresses over a fashion-plate dress, privileges an individual, handmade account of fashion over a more commercial version. By telling a story of a crystal, Lucy evoked a felt emotion through the choice of color and the transparent softness of the crystal. Modal choice is ideological, and some voices are heard more readily in some modes than others. Many young people find hip-hop or rap a space in which to make their voices heard. The tracing of those choices is an important task for educators and researchers.

An Odyssey of Self: The Odysseus in Manuel and Patsy

An odyssey of self took place in the third year of the research project introduced in Chapter 5 (see also Appendix A). Students involved in the study are the same population in the support English class at Princeton High School. In the fall semester, rather than have students write narratives about valued artifacts, Jackie Delaware, Jamie Frutig (student teacher), and I (Jennifer) asked 20 freshmen to create digital stories based on Homer's *The Odyssey* (1996). The project grew out of our concern that students lacked interest in and a connection to Homer's epic tale. Students in freshman English at Princeton High School struggle with *The Odyssey*, the course text, because of its arcane verse and because it is best understood when read aloud. After reading *The Odyssey* in English class, students interwove Odysseus' journey with their own story of a journey. The digital storytelling project represented a way of going between and then bridging these two worlds. *The Odyssey* worked well for the project because students found it relatively easy to couple and render multimodal a journey that they had experienced with Odysseus' gradual and perilous journey home to Ithaca. By the end of the fall semester, most students related to Homer's tale of a journey.

The assignment began with a presentation of two examples of digital stories, one by me and one by Jamie. We talked through our choices of modes and how these choices affected meanings in the story. Then everyone in the class, including Jackie (a self-described Luddite), created a storyboard for their own story and then wrote a script for the voice-over. Once there were hard copies of storyboards and scripts, the bulk of class time was spent surfing the web for images and sounds that fit their stories. Because of our small budget for producing the short films, we had to juggle equipment, such as sharing one microphone (lent by Jamie) and two Flip cameras. Even within these budgetary and technological constraints, students created impressive films worthy of accolades.

In regard to the research component of this project, which was ethnographic in its approach (Green & Bloome, 1997), I brought an emic perspective to the data collection. I live around the corner from the school, have a child at the local elementary school, and am involved in school events. To complement reflexivity and ethnographic observations, I conducted interviews with all of the students involved in the study, asking such questions as the following:

- What do you like to do outside of school?
- What is your most valued object?
- What do you like about English class?
- What do you struggle with in English?

- Do you speak other languages?
- Tell me about your interests.

Once again, what continues to impress and at first surprised me was the eclectic nature of interests these teenagers have, from cooking to skateboarding to sculpting. As evidence, here are two case studies of digital stories, one by Manuel Cordoba and one by Patsy Flores.

Manuel Cordoba. Manuel is 14, a freshman at Princeton High School. Manuel was shy and reserved at the beginning of the project but steadily became more animated as the semester went on.

Manuel admires *The Odyssey* and how Odysseus makes a long journey, faces adversities and adversaries, and triumphs in the end. Despite this, Manuel did not know how to translate his interest in the epic into prose. When I spoke with him about the project, he said:

> Well, when I thought about it, I thought kind of about what I do the most. I thought of sports because I like to play sports all the time and sports are a big part of my life, so I was thinking about how many sports I've played. I have these three main sports that I play, which are basketball, football, and soccer, and there are eighteen slides, so I could divide it into six. I divided by three, and there were six slides for each, which fit perfectly. That's what I wanted to do. (December 13, 2008)

First, Manuel created a storyboard of his digital story, which set out the modal structuring of the slides, designating the structure for his visuals, his voice-over, his fade-ins and fade-outs. This process opened up new ways for him to sediment a ruling passion, childhood memories, and cultural narratives into the text. Writing a script for the voice-over opened up the meaning-making process and allowed him to find visuals to match the story and a transition from his own sedimented identity into a literary text.

As I observed Manuel over the course of 6 weeks, there was a shift in his attitude from the first day to the last day of the project. Manuel's initial reluctance dissipated as he conceived his story, gathered visuals, and recorded his voice-over. Most of the time he sat in a far corner of the computer lab, quietly working on his story. Half of his digital story showcased scenes of soccer, basketball, and football games and the other half of his digital story featured the story of Odysseus. The voice-over that accompanied a visual of football action is as follows:

> With football, my speed was really good and I was a good catcher. I broke my ankle during practice, which really stunk because I never

got to play any game. My favorite team is the Eagles, and my favorite player is Kevin Curtis, who is a wide receiver.

The voice-over goes on to describe Manuel's love of sports in relation to Odysseus' journey and the challenges that Odysseus faced. In particular, he talked about Poseidon and "how he gave Odysseus a hard time." Then he discussed the Cyclops in *The Odyssey* as another challenge that Odysseus faced.

Manuel concluded his digital story with a retrospective look at challenges he had faced to date in his pursuit to be an athlete, such as an incident in which neighborhood kids bullied him and how the Athena (a silent, benevolent goddess who protects Odysseus) in his life is his brother: "I think that the Athena in my life was my brother in a way. I always liked to play with him and I tried to impress him a lot, so when he said I suck, I tried harder, so he boosted my chances of doing well in a sport." At this moment, Manuel transfers his interest in and connection with *The Odyssey* into a text. Relational learning transpires at this moment in the digital story, and it allows Manuel to take ownership of his learning, relate to it, and interweave his own story with Odysseus' journey. Visuals, sounds, and most of all his own voice as the dominant mode sediment Manuel's identity into a text. The digital story displays strong literacy skills, such as creating a visual and conceptual arc to his argument, but Manuel also offers one of the most effective models of interweaving Odysseus' story with his own.

Patsy Flores. Patsy, also 14, is small in stature but has a huge presence in the classroom. Patsy is friendly and exuberant, and everyone likes and values her in the group. From the beginning, Patsy knew that she wanted to focus on fashion and her dream and ultimate journey of becoming a fashion designer. Patsy described to me how she came up with her idea for the digital story: "Well, I thought of some ideas that had to do with *The Odyssey*—like adventure. I thought about fashion because that's an adventure to me. Some people may not take it seriously, but I do."

Patsy hopes one day to attend the Fashion Institute of Technology (FIT) in New York City. Her digital story begins with a quotation about fashion as an abiding philosophy of her life and her journey. This reads, "Everyday is a fashion show and the world is your runway." After talking about New York City and FIT as a muse for her designing, Patsy presents a series of photographs of rick-rack dresses that her mother made (see Figure 6.1). In this way, Patsy sediments parts of herself in with popular culture and new media images. At one point in her digital story, Patsy showcases her "sweet 15," which is a cultural spin on the North American version of "sweet 16." Her dresses vary. They range from simple, childlike dresses with blue and

Figure 6.1. Rick-rack dresses as part of everyday.

white rick-rack to much more ornate creations designed for parties. Each dress has a history, and is tied to the color, the material, the choices around the making of the dress. After presenting her childhood dresses, Patsy showcases a series of inspirational designers such as Coco Chanel. Patsy talks about how Coco Chanel began by making hats and then moved into clothing. In her story, Patsy talks about "hanging out at FIT" because she can see herself one day being a designer. In her digital story, Patsy relates her journey to Odysseus' journey because Odysseus went "from place to place and I compare myself because I plan to travel from place to place as I become known. Just as Odysseus' desire was to come home, my desire is to be famous." So much in Patsy's digital story is an expression of habitus, from her own childhood dresses to pictures of designers.

These students learned that the story of Odysseus was relevant in that their journeys, now inscribed in the digital stories, were as alive and valuable as those of the long-ago Greek heroes. They could place their texts alongside *The Odyssey* and then understand the work with new eyes. Literacy was inscribed in these stories, in the narratives they told, in the use of particular scripts and stories.

My Family, My Story: "Super Girl" Lucy

As explained in Chapter 3, I (Kate) conducted the My Family, My Story project in partnership with a local museum and a community primary school in the North of England (see Appendix A). Teachers in the school wanted to develop ways in which children who were quiet in class could improve their speaking and listening skills. The project was conceived in the context of the school's learning strategy and its focus on speaking and listening. The aim was for five families with their children, all identified as being in need of support for these skills, to create digital stories about their favorite objects.

The research component of the project involved my observing each session and writing fieldnotes. Where possible, I made digital audio and video recordings. The children also made digital audio recordings and films of each session. I tried to look at the project from the perspective of the class teacher; the museum educator; and the families, both parents and children. I recorded the process of creating the digital stories as well as the actual stories. In particular, I studied one family in depth, Lucy and her children. Lucy brought her four children to the sessions, and each child was part of the meaning-making process. My focus was on the stories and how they expanded over time.

Overview of the Project. The project was carried out in six sessions:

1. The families were introduced to the project and started to think about their special objects. They created an All About Me storybox to decorate and took home disposable cameras to take pictures of their special objects.
2. The families continued to decorate their storyboxes as well as make All About Me films.
3. The families created timelines of their family life.
4. The families scripted and then created videos of their talking about themselves and their special objects.
5. The families described their shoeboxes and also talked about the photographs they had taken. They told stories associated with the objects in the photographs. Recordings of special stories were made, using digital equipment.
6. The recordings of the stories were checked and redone if necessary.

A key element in the process of creating the stories was attention to the quality of the recordings. To achieve this, families were encouraged to film in separate rooms. In the case of Lucy's family, the film included interaction between all of the family members. Families rehearsed and then filmed their stories over time. Stories were extended through creating storyboards, writing out stories, and rehearsing the stories using digital audio and video media. The process of creating the stories was not instant, and one key finding was that by giving the families time to script, create, and rehearse the stories, the stories were improved.

The project involved a number of modalities. First, participants created mini storyboxes using pen, paper, and cardboard. Then they used craft materials to create shoeboxes in which they placed special objects. The use of disposable cameras allowed participants to talk about special objects in their homes. The use of digital audio enabled the children to listen carefully to their parents. Film was useful to record all the activities and the My Family, My Story videos. Lucy's family in particular filmed family members telling stories about each other. They had to really listen to each other to make sure the sound quality was high, and many stories were recorded several times to get them right.

Lucy's Digital Story. Lucy said at the beginning of the project, as we shared artifact stories, "My name's Lucy, and my favorite object is my children because they are always there for me." In the first session, Lucy and her children sketched out their special home, with her daughter adding to the discussion and clarifying her mother's choices:

> LUCY: Right: [I took my] children. I like to listen to music. I love
>   biscuits [laughs]. That's me two bears.
> JANE (her daughter): She has got a massive one.
> LUCY: I like to have dolls.
> JANE: She has got loads in the house.
> LUCY: That's me on the phone: I like to talk to my friends [image of
>   phone]. I do a lot of hovering and washing—exhausting [image
>   of sad face].

> Lucy told me that she would not keep going at all if it were not for
> her children. She looked quite despairing. (Fieldnotes, November 24,
> 2008)

The images in Lucy's minibox show a phone and musical notes and five minifigures, all lined up. This began Lucy's story, but at that point it was expressed only through the modality of drawing, without color. When Lucy came back with her photographs taken at home, she was more specific. Here she is talking about the images she took: "I took pictures of my two birds, of my candles. I have got a quartz stone. I took a picture of the [bear]. Jane took a picture of the candle" (Digital audio tape, December 8, 2008).

Lucy's daughter Jane (9 years old) interviewed her about the crystal:

> JANE: What kind of photos did you took on the camera that hasn't
>   been developed yet?
> LUCY: I took my candles and I took my two bears and I took my
>   quartz stone, which is a pink stone [see Figure 6.2].

Figure 6.2. Lucy's crystal.

JANE: Is it kind of like a crystal?
LUCY: Yes.
JANE: Anything else?
LUCY: My children. I think I took my children.

As Lucy became more engaged in the project, she began to reveal more of her life. In the final session, this interview was recorded and filmed by Jane:

> LUCY: I got this crystal off my friend because I have had a hard time
> in the last couple of years and she thought it would help and
> because I had that one I collect a few little ones as well.
> JANE: Does it help?
> LUCY: No [long pause, laughter] . . . it looks nice! (long pause)
> JANE: Does it feel special to you?
> LUCY: Yes, because my very close friend gave me it.

The children made up questions and created a montage of emotional accounts of each other's attributes, which were cut in together in the final story. Lucy's two children recorded this piece of film, in which her older daughter, Jane, interviewed her older son, Henry:

> JANE: How many people are in your family?
> HENRY: Five
> JANE: Who are they?
> HENRY: Me, Jane, Mum, C, and L.
> JANE: How old are they?
> HENRY: Mum's 27, Jane's 9, I am 7 nearly 8, L's 1, and C's 2.

JANE: What are they like?
HENRY: C's cheeky, L's cheeky, Jane's moody, I'm lazy, and Mum's
SUPER GIRL!!!

Lucy's digital story was layered with her own experience of her children, of her objects, and of her journey through a difficult time. This experience was represented multimodally—that is, in interaction and through the aesthetic properties of the quartz crystal, which created affect. It was also evoked through the interviews the children did and in the layering of these interviews. The final story included the words *Super Girl* in a special font, which really lent a dramatic feeling to her son's statement.

This project showed that gathering together everyday stories and then drawing on practices, such as interviews, to make a digital story was a powerful experience in relation to identity. Lucy and her family, by sedimenting their identity in this digital text, created a multimodal text that was ideologically infused. It was created in response to a number of choices about color, shape, and inflection that enabled meaning to be co-constructed and shared across the domains of home and school.

Literacy can be a connected experience of telling stories that are then realized multimodally but lead to great power and agency in the classroom. When Lucy's children showed their digital story in their classroom, they became more confident learners. The presentation of digital stories is a powerful aid to literacy and a way to create more agency in other domains of practice.

DIGITAL STORYTELLING AS ARTIFACTUAL LITERACIES: UNPACKING THE PROCESS

Having presented three examples of the effectiveness of digital storytelling, we now want to examine what happens when we make texts. First, they are shaped by the habitus, the acquired dispositions over time. As explained in Chapter 1, the habitus constructs everyday routines and practices. These can then produce stories located within time and space. Out of these stories come shaped texts. These texts themselves then transform the habitus. Hence the circle shown in Figure 6.3.

Patsy's digital story, described above, was of her childhood dresses, of their color and shape, of their modalities. She infused these images into her digital story. The stories told in homes are shaped by the people in this chapter into texts, which are digital. They appear as visual plus oral; as pieces of film, with gesture; as images in photographs; as stories told and retold and made new in the digital context. When digital storytelling

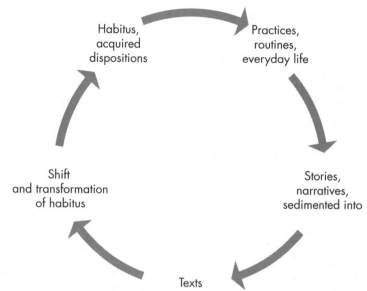

Figure 6.3. The circle of meaning making.

enters the circle, the circle looks different and has new dimensions, as outlined in Figure 6.4.

In this figure there is much more going on. First, the story has to be created through discussion and interaction. The acquired dispositions need to be invoked. The story can be created through a storyboard or rehearsed. Then the story needs to be shaped digitally. Digital audio equipment or video can be used to record the story. Following that, images need to be photographed and scanned to accompany the story, and the choice of those images is critical. Music and sound can be chosen to create effects, and particular fonts used. The range of modalities is greater, and the choices available to the sign maker are widened. We draw on Kress's (1997) theory of the motivated sign, which is shaped by the interest of the sign maker. We are concerned to trace that interest, to give it agency, and to consider how by tracing back the interest, we can motivate meaning makers.

Let us unpack the elements of digital storytelling, moving from the everyday in meaning making, to the need for connectivity in learning, to the multimodal dimensions of the digital story. Digital storytelling can be seen as an ideologically shaped practice, in that the modal choice is imbued with previous encounters with form and culture. Once these elements are considered, digital storytelling gets more complex.

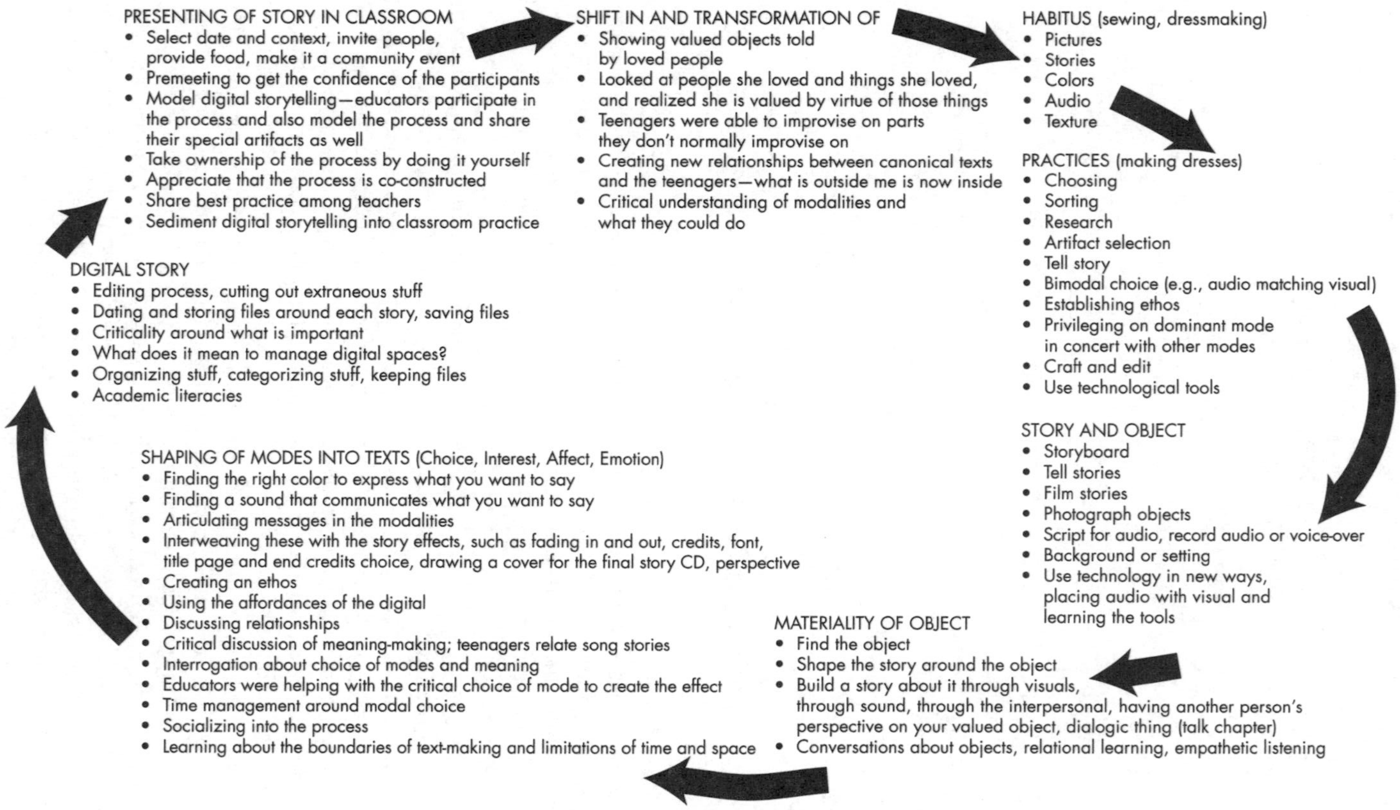

PRESENTING OF STORY IN CLASSROOM
- Select date and context, invite people, provide food, make it a community event
- Premeeting to get the confidence of the participants
- Model digital storytelling—educators participate in the process and also model the process and share their special artifacts as well
- Take ownership of the process by doing it yourself
- Appreciate that the process is co-constructed
- Share best practice among teachers
- Sediment digital storytelling into classroom practice

DIGITAL STORY
- Editing process, cutting out extraneous stuff
- Dating and storing files around each story, saving files
- Criticality around what is important
- What does it mean to manage digital spaces?
- Organizing stuff, categorizing stuff, keeping files
- Academic literacies

SHAPING OF MODES INTO TEXTS (Choice, Interest, Affect, Emotion)
- Finding the right color to express what you want to say
- Finding a sound that communicates what you want to say
- Articulating messages in the modalities
- Interweaving these with the story effects, such as fading in and out, credits, font, title page and end credits choice, drawing a cover for the final story CD, perspective
- Creating an ethos
- Using the affordances of the digital
- Discussing relationships
- Critical discussion of meaning-making; teenagers relate song stories
- Interrogation about choice of modes and meaning
- Educators were helping with the critical choice of mode to create the effect
- Time management around modal choice
- Socializing into the process
- Learning about the boundaries of text-making and limitations of time and space

SHIFT IN AND TRANSFORMATION OF
- Showing valued objects told by loved people
- Looked at people she loved and things she loved, and realized she is valued by virtue of those things
- Teenagers were able to improvise on parts they don't normally improvise on
- Creating new relationships between canonical texts and the teenagers—what is outside me is now inside
- Critical understanding of modalities and what they could do

MATERIALITY OF OBJECT
- Find the object
- Shape the story around the object
- Build a story about it through visuals, through sound, through the interpersonal, having another person's perspective on your valued object, dialogic thing (talk chapter)
- Conversations about objects, relational learning, empathetic listening

HABITUS (sewing, dressmaking)
- Pictures
- Stories
- Colors
- Audio
- Texture

PRACTICES (making dresses)
- Choosing
- Sorting
- Research
- Artifact selection
- Tell story
- Bimodal choice (e.g., audio matching visual)
- Establishing ethos
- Privileging on dominant mode in concert with other modes
- Craft and edit
- Use technological tools

STORY AND OBJECT
- Storyboard
- Tell stories
- Film stories
- Photograph objects
- Script for audio, record audio or voice-over
- Background or setting
- Use technology in new ways, placing audio with visual and learning the tools

Figure 6.4. The circle of digital storytelling.

The Everyday in Meaning Making

Educators are increasingly looking for ways in which they can honor home experience in their work. The word *habitus* can signal home experience, everyday experience that is sedimented into practices. A link to habitus is important in that this levers far more meanings. If meaning makers strongly invest their habitus in meaning making, they are more inclined to be more deeply engaged in what they are doing. Texts with this historical rootedness in the habitus have a longevity, as they go back to experiences and practice from other domains. Connecting domains of practice enables students to move forward.

Connectivity as Learning

Connecting domains of practice involves what we have identified as *relational learning*. This is learning that transforms material from one domain to another but has connectivity across domains. For example, in a book-making project a teacher brought in jean pockets from home and the children put objects in the jean pockets, making a pocket book that instantiated home practice but became a storybook in the day-care center (Whitty et al., 2008). Relational learning is a process that happens over time. Both the projects we describe in this chapter took place over a period of about 3 months. Meaning making is iterative, and although we focus on moments of meaning making, we also see it as a process by which identities are sedimented into the various modal aspects of the digital stories.

Barton and Hamilton (1998) documented the literacy practices of a community. This kind of work informs our theorizing about these digital stories, because it was the tracing of practices across domains and the identification of literacies in different domains of practice that we found helpful when looking at the stories. Patsy placed a number of domains of practice (e.g., fashion, home sewing, her cultural experiences, her friendships) into a seamless textual collage that uniquely showcased her "ruling passions." Barton and Hamilton found that people in community contexts carry these passions within them. It is this eclectic placement of these passions, realized in these modalities, that makes the text particularly meaningful to Patsy. Meaning makers produce these texts, guided by their multiple interests and passions and then infusing multiple modalities, and consumers read these complex texts. The production of the text shift both the meaning maker and the context in which the text is made. It distributes meaning. The fractal shards of identity become vibrant through sounds, visual images, and other modalities such as color and shape.

Multimodality and Digital Stories

Digital stories have their own texture, but they draw on multiple modes (Kress, 1997). They weave together sound plus image, which may be of a three-dimensional object, thus making the digital story thicker. Visual and other sensory memories of the event activate habitus. For example, Patsy's images of her dresses activate her experience of making dresses. The sensory world is evoked by the digital. That multimodal sense and those memories of an event are thrown into relief when a child creates a text or Patsy creates a digital story. Our life histories give different meanings to our readings. Only when Manuel wove his own life history, represented by his football story, together with *The Odyssey* could he comprehend the text. Kress and van Leeuwen (1996) argue that meaning is always tied to the personal and the affective and that the production and communication of meaning is always affective and constitutive of subjectivity. Cultural histories determine text-making. It is the cultural environment that determines what is available to the child. Digital stories are "bricolages"—they are ways in which the world is remade through texts. Kress (1997) strongly signaled that children's interests, their cultural histories, and their subjectivities were critical in the shaping of meaning. These histories, however, can only be understood through a medium such as ethnography, which is about finding context, about providing "thick description" and a layered contextual account of how choices were made and in what context, and about the history of the sign maker.

Digital Storytelling as Ideological

Street (1993, 2008) identified literacy, and then multimodality, as ideological, that is, lying within relations of power. To take an ideological approach—situating digital storytelling within the context of power of everyday life and practices—means combining the ethnographic with the multimodal. It is as much about Patsy's valuing of dresses as it is about combining photographs of famous designers as ways of expressing her habitus. It is the remixing of those components and ideological shaping into modes that then transform the text. With Lucy's family, each family member constructed interviews over time, which produced a composite family story, with qualities ascribed to children, Lucy's account of her favorite objects, and special family stories, such as the story of when her youngest child was born. The whole family participated in this text-making. The children actively created the digital text. By enabling the affordance of the children's creating the texts, new accounts and experiences from that family were let in and represented. The family became more confident, and Lucy as the mother enjoyed her family experiences as represented in her story. She moved from being down on herself (she described having the crystal given to her when she was having a bad time) to active storytelling, through modalities. The ideological nature of the multimodal offers a way of acknowledging the power of different modes to let in new kinds of meanings. Educators can harness these powerful modes when asking children to create texts.

With Manuel, reframing a text, such as *The Odyssey*, but using ideologically different material, such as football, was possible only because he was using other modalities. Music is a powerful tool for creating new kinds of spaces for text-makers. The emotional resonance of music goes beyond the space of the classroom and seeps into school. By remixing and recontextualizing out-of-school experience in his digital story, Manuel was accounting for different parts of his identity (Dyson, 2003).

REVISITING THE "HOW": MAKING IT HAPPEN

By revisiting the circle of digital storytelling, we can make the process more explicit. In Figure 6.4 we showed that process in a visual manner and considered the implications for practice. This figure helps us understand how it is possible to actually realize a digital storytelling project in the classroom. Below, we explore each stage of the process in more detail and provide suggestions to help teachers engage students in the classroom.

Activating the Habitus in Texts

The challenge for teachers is to draw on the everyday—the habitus—in teaching, to allow children to articulate their routines and practices through texts. Digital storytelling brings that alive, for example, by enabling digital photography in homes to be used to re-create the home experience. There can also be links to other experiences, to widen the experience of the everyday—for example, visiting sports sites to do research for the project or sorting images from home for the story.

Crafting and Practicing Story Making

The families practiced telling stories as they worked toward their digital storytelling. They needed quiet spaces to hear stories and needed to spend time deciding which stories were important. The project team spent time with children and parents crafting particular shared stories and making them bigger. There was also the issue of getting acquainted with the digital and drawing on existing practice. There is also a need to describe the relationship between the story and the object when crafting stories around objects.

Using storyboards can help activate artifacts and stories, as can telling stories while holding up the artifacts. In the My Family, My Story project, children filmed their parents talking about their favorite objects. In the high school project, the teenagers put the photographs of their object plus the digital audio recordings of the story together. They spent time choosing songs to accompany their stories. To create a finished script, they scripted their voice-overs.

Objects as Evoking the Sensory World

In digital storytelling, objects are materialized in a digital form. Patsy's dress or Lucy's crystal appear on screen, with voice-over accompanying the image. The pink of the crystal or the color of the dress instantiate particular previously experienced emotions. The objects have auras, traces associated with past practice and choices from the habitus. The sensory nature of the object, its feel and texture, is evoked in the digital form. Color, shape, and texture, as well as past history, shape the choices around the objects. In the digital storytelling world, material objects open up emotions. Teachers can look at an object and then help their students build a story about it through having another person's perspective on their valued object. Conversations about objects are vital to create both relational learning and empathetic listening. Extended questioning about objects or even simple questions like "Did it help?" can expand stories. Through talking, stories expand and grow, and by asking about the material qualities of an object, teachers can bring more to life.

For example, in the Every Object Tells a Story project (described in Chapter 3), students spent time experiencing the sensory qualities of an object—its texture, feel, shape, and color—before playing a guessing game about an object. Educators brought in mystery objects in a soft bag and asked students to hold objects and try and guess what they were from their feel. Students also brought in objects and asked other students to make links between the objects and the person. From this activity, writing that described objects could be elicited.

The Shaping of Modes into Texts

In digital storytelling, modal choice is decided through a shaping process. The process of digital storytelling is about articulating messages in the modalities—for example, in the visual—and then interweaving these with a story. Meaning makers choose modes, such as sound or visuals, according to their interests. Some modes are more laden with sense—music can carry a person to a different world. Modal choices are historically driven—some teenagers will use music rather than words to suggest a feeling. Teachers can then help students find a sound and the right color to express what they want to say. Conveying these meanings across modalities, from visual to sound, can be very powerful. Choices are also laden with ideologies. For example, Patsy's choice of Coco Chanel was laden with ideological richness and meaning.

The use of effects, such as fading in and out, credits, font, title page and end credits choice, drawing a cover for the final story CD, creates an atmosphere for stories that are signaled by these modal choices. In order to "thicken" digital productions, teachers can find out about using the affordances of the digital (e.g., Google Earth has an effect, as do podcasting, Facebook, television interviews, catchphrases, comedy shows, and popular culture references). Critically examining modal choices can lead to discussions around popular culture in a wider context.

Some modal choices take longer to create than others, and time management around modal choice is about learners being socialized into the process. In both projects described in this chapter, the process was messy and complex and involved learning about the boundaries of text-making and the limitations of time and space.

The Production of the Edited Digital Story

Digital stories have a beginning, a middle, and an end to fit within the genre of a story. In creating digital stories, learners need to be aware of the importance of story structure. The genre of film is also important, and in using the affordance of the digital, the creator needs an introduction, credits, and dedications. Voice-overs, which are created by the students, and still images can frame a story.

Teachers can be involved in the editing process and the ways in which cuts can be made. The storing of digital files is a huge part of digital storytelling. What is important in the mass of stuff, and the images and voice files that are created becomes a focus for the project. The practice of keeping files in different locations is also important for students to learn.

Presenting the Stories

A ceremonial event is important to mark the telling of the digital stories. Both members of the outside community—other schoolteachers as well as parents or siblings—and classmates can be invited. The feeling of a special occasion can be created. The story of the making of the stories also can be shared among a school community, and new practices can be created. The final affirmation is the process of digital storytelling sedimenting into classroom practice.

In the artifactual literacies and digital story projects that I (Jennifer) conducted at Princeton High School, community events were organized each year to celebrate student success. Community members, district administrators, the principal, guidance counselors, teacher-researchers, and I sat at tables with three students per table to listen to their presentations of multimodal portfolios or view a screening of their digital story. In the My Family, My Story project, teachers, parents, and children listened to the digital stories that were about valued objects, told by loved people. Lucy cried when she saw her story as she realized the amazing gift that her family was to her. In both projects, there was a felt sense of accomplishment among students because their teachers took the time to acknowledge their investment.

Shift and Transformation of the Habitus

The process of digital storytelling involves a thickening of a thin concept. The story of the crystal became thicker through interaction. Students have to use referential language and relational language in relating across domains. For example, Patsy's dressmaking was linked to the wider world of fashion. The students brought to their digital storytelling unconscious dispositions that were expressed through their modal choices. The projects allowed students to actively work with their own subjectivities, and they could then situate themselves in the English classroom in a way that they had not been able to before.

Relational learning was about empathetic listening by children and adults—creating new kinds of listening opportunities. Cameras became artifacts of listening—people listened more, and stories were told into an inhabited space. Because students were listened to, the habitus changed. Children asked deeper questions and thought about the answers more carefully. Outside and inside became blurred in the making of the stories.

At the same time, digital storytelling created a critical understanding of modalities and what they could do. Students thus accessed power as communicators. We need students who can create digital stories and understand the language of mode, for this gives them power. To be able to make meaning and succeed gives them power. Teaching can then become transformed practice.

Digital Storytelling as Transformed Practice

Digital storytelling is an example of transformed practice (Cope & Kalantzis, 2000). The storyteller can bring from home an artifact of identity that is about his or her ruling passions. At the same time, the artifact is transformational as it places the meaning maker in a new space. Showing digital stories to others is often a way of creating these transformations. Watching people's reactions to the stories can be a very powerful experience. Lucy's daughter Jane showed her digital story to her class, which was a separate space from the after-school environment in which she constructed the stories. This enabled her to feel proud of her family and of her achievement in creating the story.

With the project at Princeton High School, a two-way process of transformation occurred. Students built on their outside social and intellectual capital and funds of knowledge (Gonzalez et al., 2005) to produce multimodal texts, while Jackie and I (Jennifer) were taught and mentored by students about digital literacy practices, such as using Movie Maker and adding sound bites to video footage. Jamie, a teacher-in-training, earned the respect of the students by serving as our resident technology guru. The beauty of such projects is the dissolution of power dynamics and the creation of respectful learning environments.

In the school where the My Family, My Story project took place, the teachers saw the potential of this way of working. All the teachers in the school purchased Flip cameras and gave them to the children to record their learning throughout the day. The extended questions and the skills learned on the project were seen as very valuable. The importance of emotion in learning and the affective shifts in motivation through ownership of learning were strongly experienced through digital storytelling. Artifacts evoke powerful memories of loss and transformation. In digital storytelling, these come alive again. The modalities that digital storytelling involves create a much wider communicative spectrum where students can layer and laminate their identities in new ways (Holland & Leander, 2004). This lamination of identities can involve many layers and many modes. The effect on the learner, however, is transformational. The effect of creating these stories was to open up confidence and new skills sets in the learners and to create interactional moments that could only have happened through the digital story production process. Digital technologies can open up new identities and realities. In the final vignette of this chapter, Tisha Lewis movingly describes the affordances that computers open up for a mother of four in her engagement with what she described as "the motherboard." Computers are themselves artifacts that can create alternative spaces for meaning making and personal expression. They inhabit homes like other valued, special objects, and their affordance is critical in making meaning come alive. As an original contribution to this book, Tisha Lewis wrote the following vignette about her research on materiality and digital environments:

The Motherboard Stories
By Tisha Y. Lewis

Larnee, an African American single parent of four sons in her mid-30s, has a love affair with digital literacies. She uses digital literacies as a way of "connecting" with herself and others. She views digital literacies as *cells* working together in a body, similar to the way cells help the body to function. Larnee enters the digital world through gaming, instant messaging, texting and talking on her cell phone to guide and influence her decisions on a daily basis. She creates a virtual space where she is not judged by her appearance, race, education, or social status but is known and is acknowledged, through her online social networks, as a mother, friend and counselor, each having a meaningful commonality: acceptance.

The quest to obtain acceptance comes from the experience of being one of 16 siblings who was responsible for taking care of the physical needs of the family by washing clothes, cooking, and cleaning for the entire family from the time she was 5 years old. Larnee, feeling the residue from her past, remembers the emotional, physical, and verbal abuse she experienced. In addition, she was banned from attending school until she was 12 years old and was sexually abused by a family friend during her childhood. Her world is full of the pains and struggles of being unemployed, receiving government assistance, having no high school diploma, and living with a painful and rare skin disease called epidermolysis bullosa, the same disease that took the life of her younger sister many years ago. Now engaging in digital literacy practices in her home with her sons is a therapeutic ritual for her that takes her mind off her current struggles and past hurts. To her, these literacies are an extension of herself in which the practices she engages in takes over parts of her internal and her external worlds.

In telling her story to me, Larnee describes, at times vividly and graphically, the ways in which her life was shaped by digital literacies; in fact, she has a fascination with the artifact called the motherboard. The primary functional unit of the computer, the motherboard has intricate devices and tools that make the rest of a computer function properly; it is a tool she sees as the heart of the computer. Larnee attributes other functions to the motherboard, as a mother of four sons, a provider, a consumer, and an agent for change.

When Larnee explained and described the motherboard to me in 2007, she used various modalities (i.e., movements and sounds) to emphasize her meaning in unique ways as she described the equipment that she uses to make sense of her past and present histories. This example evokes the work of Turkle (1984, 2007), who argues that we should see the computer not just as a tool but as a part of our social and psychological lives. She argues that individuals' experiences with computers change the ways they think, function, and act in the world. Turkle believes that we should look beyond what the computer can do for us to how it changes what we do and also how we think. These issues became more apparent when Larnee began to talk more about the motherboard, directly applying its roles and functions as symbolic to herself, multimodality, and the body. As she spoke about the motherboard, she used nonverbal gestures (e.g., balling her hands into fists and shaking them or using them in circular motions, touching her chest) to help describe her past and present histories with the computer.

SUMMING UP: DIGITAL STORYTELLING AS ARTIFACTUAL

Patsy, Manuel, and Lucy were able to create digital stories that made new connections for them. They were intertextual, moving from home texts to popular culture texts seamlessly. Digital stories allow the creation of liminal, in-between spaces for meaning makers to make connections, evoke friendship, describe past memories, and look forward to future identities, like Manuel. They allow a scrapbook experience from the home, such as dresses, to be embedded in a textual landscape of communication in ways that might not immediately "work" in film language but create new platforms for meaning makers. These can then be developed in literacy teaching contexts.

CHAPTER 7

Teaching Artifactual Literacies

There is a very scattergun thing in my classroom. You get some classrooms that are very ordered; in my classroom the anarchy is not very far away. I like that kind of thing. You get the shelves and stuff, it is just clutter; if you pick through it, there are lots of little stories there, there is a lot going on.

—Sandy, third-grade teacher

IN THIS INTERVIEW excerpt from a third-grade classroom teacher in a school in an ex-mining community in Yorkshire in the United Kingdom, it is possible to glean an insight into the pedagogy of artifactual literacies. Teaching artifactual literacies involves blending the everyday, the messy, the material qualities of life, with stories that then create opportunities for literacy learning. From oral stories, writing and the craft of talk emerge.

We draw on work by Moje and colleagues (2004) and Guitiérrez, Baquedano-Lopez, and Tejada (1999) in exploring ways in which classrooms can act as "third spaces" for students to express their identities. We argue that bringing in home artifacts already radically alters the space of learning. If learning takes place with objects that are familiar, historical, everyday, culturally relevant, handmade, and crafted with care, the space looks different. This is important because artifacts in school (pencils, assessment materials, books, rulers, interactive whiteboards, computers, chalkboards, flip charts, lockers, and desks) are different from artifacts at home (kitchen equipment, televisions, personal stereos, sofas, comfortable spaces, beds, and places to relax). Homes and schools are different domains of practice, but when they are connected, this has consequences for teaching and learning. We argue for the power of artifacts to lever in experiences from outside school and to unite children who might have disparate experiences, creating listening opportunities between children and adults. Artifacts mediate experience in gentler ways. In sum, artifactual literacies can do the following:

- Harness popular cultural enthusiasms
- Display experiences the class members have all experienced together

- Develop interests and passions, such as collections
- Open up figured worlds of practice
- Develop powerful opportunities for talk and model-making
- Create opportunities for writing

In this chapter, we describe how teachers can create their own spaces for learning and social transformation. We start by looking at artifactual literacies at home and school, then move to classrooms. We explore the relationship between learning and artifacts. We provide a case study of teaching artifactual literacy and then move into a methodology for extending writing using artifacts. We revisit artifactual critical literacies. Finally, we end by discussing the consequences of artifactual literacy for teachers and students.

ARTIFACTUAL LITERACIES IN THE CLASSROOM: TEACHERS' PERSPECTIVES

Artifactual literacy is as much about acknowledging and incorporating valued objects and their attendant stories as it is about opening up literacy to multimodality and thinking multimodally. Artifacts carry modes, sometimes isolated but often combined modes, and these multimodal properties are as much a part of making meaning with texts as alphabetic print. Hence, multimodal properties need a language in order to be discussed, analyzed, thought about, and critically framed. To develop multimodal awareness, I (Jennifer) conducted two research studies with teacher education students (see Appendix A; Rowsell et al., 2007; Rowsell & Rajaratnam, 2005). In both studies, I asked students to think about multimodality in their teaching and learning about literacy teacher education.

Dorothy's Pedagogic Artifacts

In the first study, I shadowed and conducted interviews with Dorothy Rajaratnam, a gifted elementary school teacher. After her teacher education year, I had occasions to observe Dorothy teach and speak with her colleagues, and she is a natural teacher. Over the course of Dorothy's teacher education year, I interviewed Dorothy about her life story, her teaching experience in Sri Lanka and Montreal, and her teaching internships at two schools in the Toronto area. Part of the study involved analyzing such pedagogic artifacts as her lesson plans, her classroom designs, and anecdotal notes about her teaching and assessment. Together, we broke apart her story through the artifactual and co-wrote a chapter about the experience (Rowsell & Rajaratnam, 2005).

Artist-Teachers' Artifactual Creations

In the second study, I interviewed three artists-turned-teachers about moving from art and design to elementary school teaching. Taiga, Anjani, and Henry were artists or designers before entering teaching and had very particular ideas and opinions about design and the artifactual. During their internships, art and arts education presided over their philosophy of teaching. I interviewed each participant about their art and how it informs their teaching and shapes their identities-in-practice (Holland et al., 1998). What became clear in the study is that the three individuals used art and the artifactual to represent identity and shifts in identity. In light of the study, artifacts created by the three artists represent an embodiment of what they brought to their artists' practice, which could be described as their cultural capital (Bourdieu, 1990). I claim that "through semiotic mediation each participant came to terms with shifts in their identity. Where Taiga uses installations and three-dimensional art improvising on artistic habitus, Anjani found her medium interweaving East Indian images with digital forms" (Rowsell, 2008, p. 336).

The three artists had a felt sense of design and how art mirrors life and meaning making, and these natural, tacit dispositions serve as an overlay for their teaching and, ultimately, for student learning. All three artists actively embed arts and an artifactual approach in their teaching, which in many ways aligns more with the kinds of multimodal texts that their students use outside of school. Artifactual literacy therefore provides a bridge between "ruling passions" at home and acts as a conduit for everyday life to flow into the classroom (Barton & Hamilton, 1998).

Sandy's "Stuff"

To investigate how teachers created special spaces for children to learn using artifacts, I (Kate) was involved in a project called A Reason to Write with three artists and three teachers (see Appendix A). One of the interviews I conducted half way through the research project (May 21, 2009) was with Sandy, a third-grade teacher, in an ex-mining village school in the United Kingdom. As he took me on a guided tour of his classroom, he described how he had turned it into an artifactual space: "I asked the caretaker to put up the shelves over there last year [laughs] because I wanted the shelves for my stuff! [laughs]." Sandy's classroom can be understood as being an instantiation of his habitus. He described to me his boyhood in Scotland, saying, "I wanted to make my classroom the kind of classroom I would have liked when I was at school."

Sandy loved collecting "stuff"—at home he has a large Viking ship and what he called a "man cave" in the attic. Sandy's girlfriend got fed up with his stuff, so he took it to school. Of the shelves, he said, "A lot of the kids look at it and say where did you get that from—it is my little collection, you can kind of talk some of these through" (see Figure 7.1). Each object on the shelves was connected to a story or experience the class had shared. Sandy also shared his home experiences with the children he taught. His small son's photograph was on his desk, and displays of himself as a child filled the room. As I filmed the classroom, I discovered small objects above lightbulbs, rescued from oblivion and lovingly given a name and a place.

Sandy's classroom full of artifacts also has a purpose. His students— many of whom say they are "too old for toys"—come from a particular community that has suffered a quarter-century of disadvantage since the mining industry collapsed in the mid 1980s. For Sandy, artifactual literacy reminds the children not only of the stories they have experienced, the trips they have been on, the ruling passions in the classroom, but also of popular culture, sporting passions, different kinds of experiences—all represented in the classroom space. It also creates for the children in his classroom a team that everyone wants to belong to: "I want the kids to feel they are part of [pause] 'family' is a bit pretentious, but 'gang' is good," Sandy said.

Everyday material life inhabits this space. Many of the objects, the "stuff" of Sandy's "home as classroom," reflect his classroom's ruling passions

Figure 7.1. Sandy's shelves.

(Barton & Hamilton, 1998). Sandy has realized that artifacts can create places in his classroom where children can "at home" and feel safe. From this place of safety and connectivity, of felt connections to objects through experiences, the children in his classroom were able to learn productively.

ARTIFACTUAL LITERACIES AND LEARNING

In Chapter 2 we suggested that artifacts have the power to create listening opportunities for communities through the stories people tell. In subsequent chapters we described the power of artifacts to create new opportunities for storytelling, and we showed how these stories can be transformed into writing. In Chapter 6 we looked at digital storytelling as part of that process. Throughout, we have seen that learning in *relational* terms—that is, with teachers and students mediating artifacts together—leads to learning as a creative process of transformation. Artifacts can become semiotic in that process of mediation, as we saw in Chapter 3 when we looked at the relationship between objects and talk.

Artifacts are simultaneously ideal and material in that they include material forms within them, but their ideal nature is shaped by human intention. Activity theorists such as Lave and Wenger (1991), drawing on the work of Vygotsky (1978), argued for the role of the symbolic and the material in human cognition, thus providing a *situated* account of learning. Latour (1994) in turn provided a theory of things that looked at the connections across the human and the nonhuman to understand the relations between them. We know from actor network theory that situated learning happens in and among objects, as learning is shaped by both human interaction and by interaction with artifacts, which contain within them different affordances for learning.

Actor network theory (ANT) describes networks as "comprised of diverse materials" (Murdoch, 1998) including human and nonhuman materials. As an approach, actor network theory traces connections and movements among elements that make up networks (Law, 1999, 2003). ANT helps us to understand that individuals and organizations are agents actively working to fulfill purposes. Through networks, agents have dynamic sets of connections through which ideas and resources flow. Within this framework, there are multiple levels of networking, including social, digital, financial, textual, and spatial. This lens brings a different focus to ethnographic fieldwork, allowing researchers to trace network connections in and to the local practices, and through ANT we can see the artifactual in all facets of life.

Learning is achieved through and with objects as a matter of course. It is artifactual in its very nature. It is also a site for potentiality. Transformative learning through artifactual literacies can involve a movement from "what is" to "what might be," which is led by artifacts (Rogers et al., 2009). Artifacts create a different environment for learning, providing a different kind of content. Meaning and content are sometimes forgotten in a drive for skills; however, when we write, we draw on the meanings created in everyday life. We now move into how this can be achieved in the classroom.

TEACHING AND LEARNING ARTIFACTUAL LITERACIES

Teaching and learning artifactual literacies can be a process by which artifacts open up new worlds for students to inhabit. In the case of young children, their power can simply reside in their size, the stories they evoke, and the emotions they create. Teaching and learning artifactual literacies can involve leaving artifacts strewn in a classroom overnight for children to find the next day or making artifacts with children to use in imaginary setting. Young children can be drawn into artifactual worlds very easily; for example, large boxes provide enormously powerful spaces in which imaginative play can take place. The power of artifacts in teaching young children is undeniable.

Here we offer a case study of teaching artifactual literacies, the Reason to Write project described above. I (Kate) spent 3 months documenting a project in which artists worked alongside teachers to create new experiences for the children. The following profiles the work of Gail, a first-grade teacher, and Sally, an artist. What this case study shows is the progression from talk in the group of children Gail worked with, to the artifactual representation of that talk, to story and writing. Artifacts in this case provided the essential glue that enabled the project to take off and to create the world making that stimulated the children's imaginations.

The Giant's Footprint

Gail and Sally worked together to create an entire imaginary space for a group of children between 4 and 6 years old. I joined with the children to record the project, using Flip cameras, audio recordings, still photography, and fieldnotes. Children carried the cameras and recorded key events. Sally, as a creative practitioner and visual artist, wanted to try using giant artifacts with the children to create a new and exciting experience for them to respond to. The events began with a letter from a boy called Sammy, who said that he had received some magic beans, that he wanted to grow them, and that he needed to find out what was at the top of the beanstalk.

The children then came into the classroom to find it strewn with giant artifacts including a giant shoe, a giant pair of glasses, and a giant cup.

The discussion centered on the hugeness of the artifacts. This led to specu-
lation about the hugeness of the giant. Gail asked the children about the
giant's head:

> GAIL: Has he got a little head?
> CHILD: A big enormous head.
> GAIL: A big enormous head, a massive head? (Audio tape, March 16,
>   2009)

The children then rushed outside into the playground and wrote the words
massive and *big* with chalk on the playground. They traced around the
giant's artifacts using chalk. The move from the finding of the giant artifacts, to the talk about the giant, to the writing of the words on the playground with chalk was fluid. One of the features of Gail's classroom was
her focus on the children's talk. She sought ways to make the classroom an
equal space where all the children could be heard. She never thought that
the children were not capable of leaps of imagination. When a child suggested an idea, the class would carry it out. In an interview (June 4, 2009),
she reflected: "All of our children have got a good enough imagination, but
providing them with the opportunity for doing it, rather than telling them
what they are doing—it is giving them the chance to share their opinion."
Gail regarded the children she taught as equal partners in the learning process. She thought that "their ideas are equal to ours—if you want them to
become confident learners and develop self-esteem, you have got to provide
them with that opportunity, don't you?"

By creating a space through the giant artifacts project that the children's imagination could engage in and by listening to the children's ideas
about the giant and then acting on them, Gail and Sally provided a world
that every child could enter into on equal terms. Here, Sammy is suggesting
that they create a castle for the giant. Sammy had whispered something to
another teacher, who asked him to repeat the idea:

> EDUCATOR: Sammy, what is your good idea?
> SAMMY: We could make a castle!
> GAIL: What could we make the castle with?
> SAMMY: Lego!
> GAIL: Would that make it big enough? Would the giant be able to fit
>   in if it was made from Lego?
> CHILD: We could use a box!
> GAIL: Have we got some boxes next door?
> CHILDREN: Yes

GAIL: Could we use them to build the castle? I never thought about that. Then with the cup and the sandwiches, we could have a party in the castle. I am very excited. (Audio tape, March 16, 2009)

The class then went and found the boxes and made the castle. In this example, the class acted on a suggestion from a child. The suggestion quickly became artifactual and realized in a tangible outcome. The next week, the class held a party, complete with party bags and games. As they discussed the party, they also wondered what else they should do. In the morning discussion, one of the children, Ben, suggested that they needed to make a map so they could get to the giant's house. Gail reminded them of this midmorning:

GAIL: We could decorate our bags. We could make party hats. And like Harry and Ben said we could make a big . . .
CHILDREN: Map!
GAIL: So there is lots and lots for you to be getting on with. . . . Harry, you could get sheets of paper and . . . you could start doing your own map. (Audio tape, March 23, 2009)

The resulting map helped the children see how to get to the giant's castle. Artifacts left by the giant were constantly appearing. On the first day, the giant's footprints appeared in the corridor. He also left his objects as well as a letter with the children. As Gail said, "They enjoyed it though, didn't they. I think they wanted to be part of the giant's life, and I think he became part of the class!" (Interview, June 4, 2009).

Gail noted that the children felt he was there without ever having met him, through his artifacts. The giant left traces of his presence during the week for the children to investigate. Children stepped into the giant's shoe, made of cardboard. One child lay inside the giant hat as if it were a bathtub. The children created soup for the giant, becoming bits of vegetables by wrapping themselves in different-colored material, and held a party to celebrate the giant's birthday. The giant also sent postcards from other places to thank the children for their presents.

The literacy activities from the artifactual experience of the giant were immense. The children used new vocabulary, like *massive, gigantic,* and *big,* chalking the words in the playground, writing them on a flip chart, and using them in conversation. As Gail said, "And still we are getting things like *gigantic* and *huge,* and they are applying it now in their conversations that have nothing to do with the giant" (Interview, June 4, 2009).

The experience of the huge artifacts created opportunities for new kinds of language. From this came experience, which became stories. One child used the word *massive* in his writing. Another child drew the giant's footprint (see Figure 7.2). Artifacts entered the classroom as if by magic and left traces of a mystery presence. The power of artifacts to evoke a world, to create other, "figured worlds" (Holland et al., 1998), or spaces where children can enter and emerge more richly engaged with literacy, can be used in many settings. The giant provided an imaginative space that the children could enter into. It was a "space that imagination seeks to change" (Leander & Sheehy, 2004, p. 4). The giant lived among the children, and they responded to his presence. These ways of using artifacts in schools can provoke more imaginative forms of expressive writing and have a powerful role to play in opening up imaginative spaces.

ARTIFACTUAL LITERACIES AND WRITING

Artifacts can be turned into complex tools for eliciting different kinds of writing, such as descriptive writing, narrative writing, poetry, persuasive writing, technical writing, expository writing, digital writing, and aesthetic

Figure 7.2. The Giant's shoe and footprint.

writing. In Table 7.1, we explore the affordances of different kinds of artifacts to open up different kinds of writing. This table provides examples of artifactual literacies in relation to writing projects that need tangible outcomes, and different kinds of writing can be plotted in relation to artifacts. The artifacts in Table 7.1 appear in various chapters of the book to build up a core argument about artifacts as opening up worlds that can lead to written narratives. Literacy today is more artifactual through digital media and a privileging of other modes in addition to alphabetic print. The increased presence of the multimodal signals a need to expand literacy and to have a language for the artifactual nature of texts and what the artifactual can offer literacy. Writing needs to acknowledge both artifacts and the artifactual nature of contemporary texts, and writing needs to simply be more artifactual and multimodal.

CREATING OPPORTUNITIES FOR ARTIFACTUAL CRITICAL LITERACIES

At this point, we want to return to the power of artifactual critical literacies, as described in Chapter 4, and the opportunities for critical literacy education. We argue that to successfully use critical literacies using artifacts, a perspective has to be in place that sees how material and social and cultural change happens only by interrogating how—and why—taken-for-granted practices, ideologies, and discourses come into being. Therefore, there has to be an approach that looks behind the material manifestation of cultural forms and traces their coming into being via a sociocultural and historical mode of inquiry.

In our work, we have looked at how the local interacts with the global to produce particular instances of practice. For example, in examining textbooks as traces of practice, I (Jennifer) considered how global corporate agendas became interwoven with local educational initiatives and even the subjectivities of individuals involved in the production process (see Appendix A). This intermingling of the local and the global illustrates well Brandt and Clinton's (2002) point that literacy practices can be transformed locally but are nonetheless tied to global communication systems.

I (Kate) have considered ways in which local texts, such as a child's bead map, can also describe and relate to global experiences such as migration to find work or to get married (Pahl, 2008). Artifacts are traveling global tracers of social inequalities. They tell stories of migration, loss, and displacement, and they are ways in which communities also renew themselves and find a voice. In our joint work, we have described how identities are inscribed into textual practices in ways that signal inequalities and distributions of power and control (Rowsell & Pahl, 2007).

Table 7.1. Artifacts and forms of writing.

Artifact	Forms of Writing
Stuffed animal (see Chapter 5)	**Descriptive Writing:** Sienna's account of *Finding Nemo* is an example of the descriptive genre of writing. A descriptive account demands reflection and often (but not necessarily) the first person. A descriptive voice requires: A distinct voice through prose indicators—such as turns of phrase or shorter or longer sentences. Very detailed phrases to put a picture in the reader's mind A central motif that runs throughout the narrative Figurative language Reflexivity in descriptive writing Showing instead of telling Sensory language
Pink crystal (see Chapter 6)	**Narrative Writing:** Lucy treasured her pink crystal because it reminds her of friendship and how her friends took care of her during a difficult period. The artifacts serve as a bridge into a reflective narrative that tells a story of an experience, event, feeling, or belief. A narrative voice requires: Introduction as a preface Resolution as a conclusion Reflective voice that allows the teller to share a story
Photograph of sunset (see Chapter 5)	**Poetry:** Maynor's account of the picture of a sunset given to him by his mother is very detailed, with poetic turns of phrases such as "like an orb of gold." Poetry uses evocative language such as "orb of gold" to communicate an experience or idea. A poetic voice requires: Figurative language Free verse Meter Rhyme
The motherboard (see Chapter 6)	**Technical Writing:** Tisha Lewis talked about a mother's story and used a computer's motherboard as a symbol of her journey. A motherboard sits in a computer as an informational repository. The valued object could serve as a springboard for a more technical account that clearly communicates information to a targeted reader. It is like expository writing that compels a response from readers to fulfill some sort of practice. A technical voice requires: Factual information Logical order Clear, concise language Objective point of view Uncomplicated structuring of information Domain-specific vocabulary

Hip-Hop CD (see Chapter 5)	**Expository Writing:** Jasmin's narrative about hip-hop represents a particular kind of writing: a historical account of era written in an expository voice. You can use music from a particular era or musicians, such as Elvis or the Beatles, as signaling a particular historical period. An expository voice requires:

> Gradual movement from past and early events to the
>   implications for the present
> An objective voice (i.e., not first person)
> Shift in voice to a more journalistic tone with phrases such
>   as "back in the day"
> Facts
> Taking account of historical moments

Happy World (see Chapter 5)	**Persuasive Writing:** *Happy World* is an installation of artifacts that expresses an overall sense of community and sense of belonging. The work of art persuades the viewer to read the message and take on the message. A persuasive voice requires:

> Logical argument
> Factual statements
> Persuasive techniques
> Stated beliefs
> Central message

Childhood dress (see Chapter 6)	**Digital Writing:** Patsy began her digital story with a series of childhood dresses as an improvisation of habitus. With digital writing, writers can use whatever mode best expresses meanings, the most apt choice. Visuals with sounds, or on their own, can achieve a particular effect that written words cannot express and vice versa. In digital writing, multimodality is central to creating "voice" in texts. A digital voice requires:

> Diverse modes—visuals, sounds, animation, words, color,
>   movement, font style and size
> Choice of genre of text—website, blog, meme, zine, wiki,
>   social networking site
> A central motif or symbol to express the ethos of the site or
>   the message of a text
> Hyperlinks—connecting a text with other texts

Golden elephants (see Chapter 2)	**Aesthetic Writing:** Language signifies rather than explicitly states the message. It pushes the boundaries of modalities— slightly stretching modalities. Use of sound in words, visuals, and extending writing into other modes creates the aesthetic. An aesthetic voice requires:

> Format
> Acrostic poetry
> Alliteration

Many teachers are passionate about creating learning spaces for children based on a principle of equality between students and teacher and about bringing community contexts into educational settings for social change. To achieve these goals, we propose that teachers harness artifacts to a critical literacies approach. We have drawn on Rogers and colleagues' (2009) critical literacy education framework, which focuses on four dimensions of critical literacy education:

- Building community
- Developing critical stances
- Fostering critical inquiry and analysis
- Focusing on action, advocacy, and social change

This process is circular and includes tools that can be applied to the process. One of these tools, we argue, is a pedagogy of *artifactual critical literacies*.

Building Community

Building community could include a focus on everyday routines and practices. Teachers could ask children to take pictures of everyday objects to bring into the classroom. They could find listening methodologies that united communities. One example is the project described in Chapter 2, in which schoolchildren created cultural boxes about their communities and sent them to other schools.

Building communities can be enabled through artifactual means, whether these are museum exhibitions, websites, art spaces, interventions, or provocations using artifacts or creating listening opportunities using digital tools such as digital storytelling. An artifactual critical literacy approach to building communities would target the material resources available in communities where there is a need for listening methodologies. For example, also described in Chapter 2, the Ferham Families project with Zahir Rafiq was specifically designed to show the community the valuable input the Pakistani British Asian families had given to the local community. Artifacts that could be recognized within all homes served to unite communities in the museum exhibition.

Building communities can also be used to foster listening between students and teachers so that students whose voices are less heard in the classroom can take up space. The Princeton artifactual and digital storytelling projects described in Chapters 5 and 6 lessened the gap between teacher and student because students taught teachers about what they valued and how to use digital literacy practices (e.g., how to put sound bites into Movie-Maker). In some ways, an artifactual approach to literacy created new, more equal roles for student and teacher.

Building Critical Stances

Building critical stances using an artifactual literacies approach can begin by students bringing in artifacts to interrogate using a critical literacies framework, such as shown in Table 7.2. In this chart, objects are interrogated for their meanings in relation to critical literacies and establishing a stance around objects. Different objects can be considered in relation to their value, the timescale attached to them, their production, their mode, and their relation to institutions of power. Objects become visible in different ways. In this table we consider five different objects that we have discussed in this book from a critical literacies perspective.

Taking the analysis a step further, students can relate specific objects to local or global timescales or spaces. By linking objects to timescales, the links from the local to the global can be brought to life. Stories can emerge from these links—for example, explaining why a child would need to describe his mother's country of origin using a bead map. This activity can open new ways of understanding students' identities and passions, and it can create a critical stance that values hidden literacies and identities.

Fostering Critical Inquiry and Analysis

Critical inquiry and analysis can stem from analyzing artifacts in such a way. For example, a local museum had a collection of objects that were originally collected in South Asia. The local South Asian community did not visit the museum; however, it was suggested that they could replace these objects, collected by British colonialists, with their own objects to create an exhibition that spoke about the colonizers in new ways. This proposal, Translating Objects (Pahl & Macdonald, 2008), provided a way of interrogating objects. Specifically, it asked the following:

- *What kinds of objects are selected for display in South Asian homes?* How are they grouped and shown? What kinds of stories are they used to tell about place, belonging, and cultural identity? What role do these objects play in translating information and values between generations?
- *What is involved in a museum's selection of objects for its collections and exhibitions?* How does the museum understand the pedagogic capacity of objects? And how does this relate to a museum's role in social representation, family learning, and inclusion?
- *What is involved in the 'translation' or movement of objects between a 'community' and a museum?* How are 'community' object-practices addressed by a museum? And how do museum collecting and display practices in turn shape a community's evaluation of its objects, forms of display and educational potential? (p. 1)

Table 7.2. Artifactual critical literacies.

Interrogated in relation to:	Artifact				
	Gold-sprayed elephant	Cookie tin from grandmother	Cardboard giant's shoe	Prayer beads made into a map of Turkey	Pink crystal
Value	Related to aesthetic set by the person who created or chose object	Related to person who gave objects	Related to use of object in social setting	Related to the contextual information the object gives, its place in the historical timeframe	Connected to relational purpose of object
Timescales	Could be short and/or long	Lifetime or several lifetimes	Short term	Key in locating a historical moment—migration from Turkey to London	Can be momentary or long term, related to friendship
Space	Placed in a home	Handed down from home to home	Placed outdoors, constructed indoors	Created elsewhere, made into a map at home	Came from elsewhere—maybe bought from a shop—but resides at home
Production	Polystyrene elephants made in factory in China (?)	Tin was originally made in UK	Made by artist using recycled cardboard boxes	Made on living room floor by child	Provenance unknown—from rock
Mode	Focused around visual salience of gold	Has sensory element, but memory is key	Important visual element is that it is larger than life for children	Adaptable beads, circular shape, can be moved	Hard, sensory, color, opaque quality
Relation to institutions of power	Can be related to experience of marriage practices (gender)	Link to everyday cultures (gender)	Link to children's identities as small; project funded through government	Migratory experience within global shifts of power	Personal experience of powerlessness; artifact as psychic space of power

These questions could then foster a spirit of critical inquiry and analysis around object collections in local museums. Artifacts have their own pedagogic potential in offering ways of telling stories, but they can also be placed within different settings to create juxtapositions that then inform learning in new ways. Artifacts can become pedagogic and develop critical inquiry and analysis through a discussion of these themes, introduced in Chapter 4:

- *Value*: Questioning of value in whose terms and why; interrogating of consumer culture versus home values and cultures; disputing of consumer notions of value in the marketplace
- *Timescale*: Relation to value, historical events, and personal events; discussion of dissonances between home and school timescales; consideration of what events matter to us; key historical events; creation of home timelines
- *Space*: Local and global spaces, cultural spaces, and public and private space; looking across domains of practice to value home objects in home spaces; using photography to find out more about these spaces
- *Production*: How the artifact was produced and what can we learn in relation to its production; the craft of the artifact and its provenance; the issue of the conditions of its production, globalization, and production
- *Mode*: Discussion of its feel, shape, color, aural dimensions, and which mode is most dominant in the artifactual experience
- *Relation to institutions of power*: Which discourses materialize in the artifact; how particular ideologies surface in the artifact

The movement from critical stance to critical inquiry can be afforded through a program that develops a more sustained approach to artifactual critical literacy. For example, teachers and students could create Facebook profiles. As demonstrated in Chapter 5, creating Facebook profiles of characters in literary works compels students to think in character. Who would engage in conversations in a Wall space? What is a character's favorite novel? What is his or her favorite saying? Thinking in character through contemporary social networking or digital communities of practice (Lave & Wenger, 1991) builds on skills students have developed from hours spent online using Twitter, MySpace, or Facebook. For example, what kind of photograph would a literary character choose in creating a profile? Take Holden Caulfield in Salinger's *The Catcher in the Rye* (1951): How would he arrange his profile on Facebook? What kinds of applications or games would he use? In terms of thinking artifactually, creating Facebook pages for characters forces students not only to think in terms of literary characters but also to think about stuff, objects, artifacts that they value; how they would visually mediate themselves; what kinds of multimodal rhetorical devices they might invoke to mediate their identities. Literary worlds can be investigated by combining the digital and the artifactual.

Focusing on Action, Advocacy, and Social Change

Finally, artifactual critical literacy can include a focus on social change through artifacts. For example, Rogers and O'Brien (in press) describe one parent's struggle in St. Louis to get the poisonous metal lead out of elementary schools. Darren O'Brien, a parent with a child at risk because of lead in the school building, gave a speech at a rally about the need to protect children from the lead. The campaign involved the use of artifacts to propel the campaign and form part of the evidence base. The artifacts from home that were significant in his growing awareness of and struggle to get the lead out of schools were leaflets sent by the city to parents about lead poisoning as well as the results of testing of his daughter for lead poisoning. The campaign was eventually successful, and the school district agreed to remove the lead from 25 elementary schools. These innovative practices opened the school up to a wider experience, which included bringing the community into the school as a relevant part of life. Rogers and colleagues (2009) write that "we conceptualise the space between what is and what might be as the place where learning occurs, as we move back and forth between two contexts of learning" (p. 195).

If we conceptualize critical artifactual literacies as being about creating new spaces but drawing on the old to make the new, the following ideas could be developed:

- Bringing artifactual literacies into the classroom—redesigning the classroom to reflect the reality of the outside world
- Using artifacts to create social change (e.g., developing a campaign against school closure through creating digital artifacts that tell the story of the school)
- Moving the school into the community by creating an exhibition of artifacts and stories
- Using local spaces as resources for learning and developing resources that occupy a "third space" jointly owned by parents, students, community members, and teachers

Ultimately, we recognize the power of narrative when thinking about artifactual critical literacies. The power of artifacts to open up new stories, to enable the telling of a story, and to create a space for listening has immense resonance in this field. Teaching artifactual literacies is above all about finding a place in the classroom for these stories.

CONSEQUENCES OF ARTIFACTUAL LITERACIES

As we have shown, the world of artifactual literacies connects to the everyday through the themes of time, space, value, production, mode, and power. Artifacts subtly shift the imbalances of power in the classroom through a new value system. Throughout human history, objects have been connected to value. When we place home artifacts in museums, we undo this process. We can imagine a world where every school has its own museum for its community, telling the community's stories. Timescales connected to objects provide different ways of conceptualizing time from those in "official" histories. These can open up new stories. Communities and schools can become connected through artifacts, as we saw in Chapter 2. We want to reclaim a gentler space, of "handmade literacies" (Whitty et al., 2008), in which a worn cookie tin has currency. However, we want to use these connective artifacts as a point of leverage in schooling. The question now is: What can an artifactual literacies pedagogy achieve in schools? The following could be the consequences of artifactual literacies for teachers.

Rethinking Value and Meaning

If value ascribed to artifacts is connected to the aesthetic, intergenerational, relational, or historical, these artifacts are positioned differently in cultural spaces. Relational objects could be placed in a stronger space in the curriculum. This might mean privileging experiences around and between objects as well as objects themselves. Levering experience of objects might mean storytelling projects that create spaces for students to share their object stories and display them in public spaces such as museums. A project like that, involving both stories and objects, might also need a rethinking of "the interrelated and interdependent nature of the social and the material world" (Christiansen, Hockey, & James, 2001, p. 81). Everyday material objects can be a way of going beyond talk, and the "currency" that is literacy, which is often most prized in schooling, can be rethought if the material enters the social world of schooling.

Rethinking Modal Choice

Students who make particular modal choices need to ascribe meaning and articulate the reasons for those choices. If a student chose a ballad of migration to go with a digital story, this choice of song can be articulated in a oral piece of narrative or written out. If students and teachers pull apart modal choice, it is possible to access agency and the fractal pieces of habitus inscribed within it. Teaching artifactual literacies means looking at the choices children make and the interaction between these choices. The affordances of different modes can be interrogated using critical literacy, to consider why and how particular affordances are important at particular times. Modal choices can link to the dominant voices—structured by global markets and consumer materialism—or they can be personally driven or community-focused, like the Ferham Families project, where a community value of gold was inscribed into a glass cabinet and celebrated (see Chapter 2). In privileging identities that are not always heard in modal choices, such as Patsy's account of fashion in Chapter 6, modal choice becomes not just an accepted practice but a decision-making practice subject to complex interrogation. We have seen in the examples of digital stories how fractal shards of habitus were infused, through modal choice—through decisions about the salience of color, music, or different textures—into digital stories. By "fractal shards of habitus," we are referring to bits of the everyday that become frozen or sedimented into artifacts, as stories set in time.

Rethinking Relational Learning

Artifacts have a relational purpose. From Winnicott's (1971) idea of the "transitional object" whereby a child takes a toy and it becomes both "me" and "not-me" as it travels with the child, to Csikszentmihalyi and Rochberg-Halton's (1981) idea of the "flow" that occurs in relation to objects in the home and the felt, psychic connections people have with objects, to Hurdley's (2006) description of her informants in her study telling different stories about the same objects as different parts of their identity come into being, the connective power of objects is clear. Artifacts give off an "aura" that can create new felt emotions, as in the Art, Artists, and Artifacts project described in Chapter 4. Familiar objects feel different from unfamiliar ones. Links with objects are ways of levering new identities into learning.

Objects that are familiar to children then create wider opportunities for learning (Rogoff, 2003, p. 239). Storytelling has long been a resource for transformative learning (Nelson, 2009). Its power to create shifts in consciousness and understanding is resonant across multiple domains of practice—homes, communities, faith centers, schools. With artifacts, stories become more powerful. They can act as *props* in a dramatic interlude. Children move quickly from the stimulus of a story to creating a prop for a story.

The power of these dramatic artifacts in classrooms is obvious to early-childhood educators; however, as students become older, the power of relational learning through artifacts is sometimes lost in a target-driven environment. They tend to be relegated to being props in drama or presented as art projects. Yet, drawing on the examples in Chapters 5 and 6, we argue that artifacts are immensely useful in working with teens to open up their "figured worlds" of practice (Holland et al., 1998). They can present opportunities for educators and teens to work together in more equitable ways. Complex digital artifacts, such as DVD equipment, digital photography, and digital audio equipment, can open up worlds of practice that teenagers feel connected with.

SUMMING UP: RETHINKING LITERACY EDUCATION
THROUGH ARTIFACTUAL LITERACIES

Schooling has its own materialities, its own objects and artifacts with traces of history (Lawn & Grosvenor, 2005). But these are specific. Not many artifacts in homes and schools are exactly the same or have the same context for use. If students are asked to list the artifacts in homes, and then list the artifacts in schools, the lists tend to look different. While some objects (pens, books) travel across domains, many reside solely in one domain or the other. Early-childhood classrooms often have a "home center" and include home artifacts as a way of connecting children's worlds. As children get older, these signs of home disappear. By the time children become teenagers, their school-based worlds are imbued with assessment regimes, and the signs of home might be limited to the computer in the corner of the classroom or the illicit sound of hip-hop that teenagers listen to as they work. Art classes may allow some discussion of home artifacts, as do writing and composition, but there will increasingly be no space for the outside world as teenagers are pressed into the demands of teacher-led assessment regimes.

Multimodality has been proposed as a solution to bridging the gap between in-school and out-of-school literacies because multimodality lets in the visual and allows for a wider range of meaning-making systems. But we think that for artifactual literacy, multimodality can only get us so far. Multimodality is about representation, about how language is only one mode for representing ideas and cultural thoughts. However, for example, as I (Jennifer) worked with the young people in Princeton, I walked the same paths as these teenagers, and as they told their stories, I witnessed what they brought in a sensory way. I felt and touched these experiences with them and engaged with their sensory understandings of the world, either through Maynor's sunset or paper crane or Patsy's handmade dresses. These everyday artifactual experiences were more than multimodal; we would argue that they were situated and embodied. Like Sarah Pink (2009), we have come to see that while multimodality is useful, there needs to be a sensory ethnographic understanding if we are to respect what our students bring into the classroom and what their artifactual knowledge could be.

Ecology is essential to artifactual literacy because of its situated-ness. To account for the artifactual, we need to feel connected to the local and acknowledge that these connections with the local—for example, going to the library and seeing the things on the walls, the leaflets advertising community groups alongside the books on the shelves. Ecologies can exist within homes and also within communities; different domains of meaning making hold memories, thoughts, faiths, and beliefs. For example, a young girl walks to school in an artifactual landscape with trees and buildings and a statue of a bear, which she replicates at home in the form of dioramas of cut-out paper, tape, and cardboard. Her dioramas are ways in which she honors and describes her experiences outside the home, but she also makes them within the home as artifactual microcosms of her lived experience.

We think that modal choice has to be understood as a felt, embodied, and sensory experience that is tied to identity. When Lucy first came to the My Family, My Story project, described in Chapter 6, her modal choice was one-dimensional. She used black ink to draw her experience of being on the phone and of doing the vacuuming and laundry. She made her box and put her children in the box as written names. It took her a while to create a film, with her daughter, of her pink crystal, which came alive with color, sound, and a sensory evocation of her world. Modal choice for Lucy was about opening up the different parts of her world, to represent and honor not only her children but also her friendships and her appreciation of the world and its objects in her life.

Artifactual literacy invites a two-way process into classroom spaces. For example, Jackie, the teacher in the English support class, found that her efforts to understand and plan her program around her students' lived experiences and artifacts empowered her own teaching as much as it empowered student learning. Jackie learned from students' stories through their artifacts, which repositioned pedagogic identities.

So what are the implications for literacy education? Literacy can be seen as part of ecologies that involve connectivity. Literacy should foster felt connections to modes and choice in modes. Literacy exists in artifacts, in that artifacts tell stories that can then be written. Artifacts open up spaces for listening and create reciprocity. Artifactual literacy brings students into a more agentive space in relation to meaning making that goes beyond the digital into the embodied, sensory, and everyday. It widens what we understand to be the life-world experience of students and allows for a much more collaborative and participatory mode of teaching and learning to come into literacy education. Artifactual literacy is about exchange; it is participatory and collaborative, visual and sensory. It is a radical understanding of meaning making in a human and embodied way.

Our Research Studies

Below, we present a chart of the different studies we have worked on that we have drawn upon in this book. These studies, while all different, all had the theme of the relationship between stories and artifacts, and they are linked in a number of ways.

(*continued overleaf*)

Kate Pahl's Research

Name of project	Place of project, funding source	When and how long?	People in project	What did it do?	Publications
Ephemera, Mess, and Miscellaneous Piles: Texts and Practices in Families	Three homes in London, UK King's College, London	1999–2003 4-year study	Kate Pahl	This study was an ethnographic study of three boys and their meaning making in three London homes.	Pahl (2003, 2004, 2005, 2006, 2007b, 2008)
Capturing the Community	Barnsley, South Yorkshire, UK Creative Partnerships, UK	2005–2007 2-year study	Kate Pahl, Heads Together, and Sally Bean	This study was an ethnographic study of the impact of a group of artists on the work of children in a school in Barnsley.	Pahl (2007a, 2009, 2010)
Ferham Families	South Yorkshire, UK Arts and Humanities Research Council Diasporas Migration Identities Research Fund	2006–2007 1 year, 3 months	Kate Pahl, Andy Pollard, and Zahir Rafiq	This project created a museum exhibition, Ferham Families, from ethnographic interviews with five family members of families who migrated to the UK from Pakistan in the 1960s.	Pahl (2010), Pahl & Pollard (2008), Pahl, Pollard, & Rafiq (2009)

Project	Location/Funder	Dates	People	Description	Resources
Every Object Tells a Story	South Yorkshire, UK University of Sheffield	2008 3 months	Kate Pahl, Zahir Rafiq, Abi Hackett, Jacqui Lindsay, and Parven Akhter	This project created a learning resource pack for family learning educators together with a website. The materials were given a trial in Sheffield, UK.	Every object tells a story pack: www.everyobjecttellsastory.org.uk
Art, Artists, and Artifacts	Leeds, UK Arts Council, UK	2007–2008 1 year	Steve Pool, Kate Genever, Kate Pahl, Lou Comerford Boyes, and Artemis Collection, Leeds	This project was about the two artists and their responses to the artifact collection in Leeds, called Artemis, which lends objects to schools for learning purposes.	
My Family, My Story	Thirsk, North Yorkshire, UK Museums, Libraries and Archives Council, UK	2008–2009 3 months	Kate Pahl, Jenny Wells, and The World of James Herriot Museum	This was a digital storytelling project that worked with five families to create five digital stories. A museum and a school were involved.	
A Reason to Write	South Yorkshire, UK Creative Partnerships, UK	2009–2010 3 months in year 1; 3 months in year 2	Kate Pahl Steve Pool	This was a small-scale project to look at the impact of a group of artists on children's reasons to write in a school in the Dearne Valley in South Yorkshire.	

Jennifer Rowsell's Research

Name of project	Place of project, funding source	When and how long?	People in project	What did it do?	Publications
Texts as Traces of Social Practice	Canada and United Kingdom	1998–2001 4-year study	Jennifer Rowsell	This study was an ethnographic-style study of the educational publishing industry.	Rowsell (2003a, 2003b, 2006a)
Multimodality and New Literacy Studies as a Lens for Learning and Teacher Education	Toronto, Canada, OISE/UT School–University Seed Grant	2002–2004	Jennifer Rowsell, Dorothy Rajaratnam, Judy Blaney, and Marianna Diiorio	There were three different studies within the overall program: an in-depth look at one teacher, Dorothy Rajaratnam, and her multimodal way of understanding her literacy program and pedagogical space; an ESL/New Literacy Studies study that looked at how cultural practices became instantiated in teaching; and a study on three artists-turned-teachers and how their understanding of art and design informs their teaching.	Pahl & Rowsell (2005), Rowsell (2003c), Rowsell & Rajaratnam (2005), Rowsell, Sztainbok, & Blaney (2007)
Family Literacy Experiences	Toronto, Canada, OISE/UTSchool–University Partnership Grant	2003–2005 2-year study	Jennifer Rowsell, Marianna Diiorio, Kathy Broad, and Mary Lynn Tessaro	The study, based on focus groups and interviews, looks at the family literacy practices of eight families and the stories of their grade-four child.	Rowsell (2006a, 2006b); Rowsell & Booth (2005)

Project	Location / Funding	Date	Researchers	Description	Citation
Screen Pedagogy	New Jersey and Maritime Province, Canada	2004–2006	Jennifer Rowsell and Anne Burke	This study looked at 20 middle school students in Canada and the US and aspects of their digital reading and writing. The study used multimodal and multiliteracies pedagogy for its heuristic frame.	Burke & Rowsell (2008a, 2008b)
Artifactual English	Princeton, New Jersey, Rutgers Council Research Grant	2006–2010 3-year study	Jennifer Rowsell, Julie Dunham, Courtney Crane, Barbara O'Breza, and Doug Levandowski	This project was an ethnographic-style research study looking at the artifactual lives of 60 teenagers using interviews, observations, and artifactual collection and analysis as the main mode of data collection and analysis.	Rowsell (2009)
Parents' Networks of Information About Literacy and Development	Adelaide, Australia, and Princeton, New Jersey, Australian Research Council Discovery Grant	2006–2010 3-year study	Sue Nichols (principal investigator), Helen Nixon (principal investigator), Jennifer Rowsell (partner investigator), and Sophia Rainbird	This project takes an ethnographic, ecological, and geosemiotic perspective on how parents develop networks of information within three quite different communities in Australia and the United States.	Nichols, Nixon, & Rowsell (2009)
Production Literacies	United Kingdom, Canada, Asia, and, the United States (individuals living in these different places), Rutgers Council Grant	2006–2009	Jennifer Rowsell and Mary P. Sheridan	This project was an interview-based research study looking at 30 producers of new media and digital technologies.	Sheridan & Rowsell (2010)

Our Way into Artifactual Literacies: A Personal Journey

Throughout this book we interweave our research with artifactual literacies as an approach to teaching literacy and as a methodology. Thus, we regard our journey into artifactual literacies as an artifact in itself that needs to be foregrounded to appreciate the genesis of the approach.

In Chapter 1, we delineated some of the material we read in order to understand the world of objects in homes. We brought these ideas back to the field of literacy and education. We then applied the ideas to communities and neighborhoods as the means to inform education. We also gained from Hicks (2002) the idea of the importance of infusing our reading into the text in order to create an intertextual account of reading and a story of our reading, in relation to literacy and artifacts. Our histories are shaped not only by our reading but also by our ruling passions, our enthusiasm for our work and for the reading that informs it. For example, we continue to draw on the idea of "ruling passions" that informs literacies (Barton & Hamilton, 1998).

Kate's Story

I (Kate) learned from Raymond Williams (1958, 1989) that texts are part of culture, that they sit within social contexts that themselves are subject to deep and sometimes unexpressed structures of feeling. Within texts such as the 19th-century industrial novel in England are the lived realities of everyday life. By linking texts to cultural practice, these novels come alive with the histories and identities of their creator. Texts are also linked to social class and tied to power relations. I appreciated, in my work as an outreach adult literacy worker, that there was something key in Williams's (1961) ideas about the need to articulate a "structure of feeling" that embodied the experiences of marginalized groups. I then encountered the work of Shirley Bryce Heath in *Ways with Words* (1983), which addresses my training as an adult literacy tutor, how this shaped my practice, and how different communities have different "ways with words." Like Jennifer, this encounter with literacy as an everyday, situated practice had profound implications for me as I worked with parents to provide opportunities for them to tell their stories (Bird & Pahl, 1994). Drawing on the work of David Barton (1994), in particular his work on the ecology of literacy, I was able to connect my work in adult literacy in everyday settings with the insights from the New Literacy Studies that literacy could be regarded as an everyday local practice, tied to social practices and identities.

For me, as for Jennifer, Gunther Kress's work in the mid 1990s came as a hugely helpful intervention, providing as it did an account of meaning making that included a far wider range of modalities and affordances (Kress, 1997). I then observed the meaning making of young children in an inner-city nursery setting. My book *Transformations* (Pahl, 1999) extended Kress's theory to the everyday world of the kindergarten setting, and by closely observing children's writing and drawing, I could observe the transformations across modes that children were taking in their work. Drawing on the work of Anne Haas Dyson (1993), I was able to observe how contextualized children's compositions were, combining drawing, writing, gesture, and action in complex multimodal texts that were richly strewn with the voice-imbued neighborhood worlds the children inhabited.

I then focused on an in-depth ethnographic study of young boys at risk of exclusion from school (see Appendix A). I was interested in the rich patterns of meaning making in their homes, and in the course of my 3-year research, I uncovered a wealth of "ephemeral literacies" in homes, included drawings and writings pushed under mattresses, made of tissue paper, destroyed, thrown away, or lost (Pahl, 2002). I found a strong relationship between narratives and objects that led to an interest in how objects relate to and instantiate narratives in home settings (Pahl, 2004).

Jennifer's Story

While studying English literature, I (Jennifer) learned that texts are interleaved with other texts and that they carry the residue of people, histories, and objects that came before them. Novels like Virginia Woolf's *To The Lighthouse* (1927/1977) bear traces of not only her own story but also texts that strongly affected her writing, and these intertexts can be found in her writings. My fascination with texts as traces of identities, histories, social practices, and intertexts affected my training as a teacher of foreign languages. The pedagogy that I studied during my year of teacher training felt like a toolbox, reifying how we learn language. The teacher-training lens that I experienced did not at all correspond with my experience studying English literature, viewing texts as historicized, textured, and, perhaps most of all, subjectively crafted. As a result of that experience, I returned to books, only this time I edited them in a publishing company, and they were not novels and poems—they were textbooks. One of my first epiphanies about the nature of "reading texts" happened when I found myself editing a spelling textbook that merged disparate, ideologically contested concepts about language development into one text. The fascination derived from how ideas in textbooks carried complicit and conflictual ways of viewing language as simultaneously open and inclusive but also skill-based and rote. How is it possible at one moment to gather family objects and spell the words, and in the next to memorize the spellings of words and call them out to a classmate? These are two different acts with different aims, different assumptions, and different models of learning.

I later appreciated this disguising process, which Bruno Latour (1987) describes as "blackboxing"; that is, how messier bits of understanding get put into a blackbox, therein made a fact, stable, closed, whole, uncontested. Admittedly, it was years later that I learned such a term and that others had identified it, but the process of working in a corporation and naturalizing the same intertextuality I had studied as an undergraduate and graduate powerfully affected how I interpreted reading and writing. That is, an epiphany about textbooks as technologies of learning that carry contested, blackboxed discourses and ideas materialized in modes led me into graduate work in literacy education with Brian Street. There was nothing predictable about this succession of events except for an abiding interest in texts, their properties, their producers, and the stories of their making.

Our stories are therefore embedded in this book, as are our engagement with families, young people, and teachers. We wish to bring them alive through examples of the power of an artifactual approach to literacy.

References

Appadurai, A. (1996). *Modernity at large: Cultural dimensions of globalization.* Minneapolis: University of Minneapolis Press.

Back, L. (2007). *The art of listening.* Oxford, UK: Berg.

Bakhtin, M. M. (1981). *The dialogic imagination: Four essays* (M. Holquist, Ed., C. Emerson & M. Holquist, Trans.). Austin: University of Texas Press.

Baldwin, J. (1948). The Harlem ghetto. In J. Baldwin, *Notes of a native son* (pp. 57–72). Boston: Beacon Press.

Bartlett, L. (2005). Identity work and cultural artefacts in literacy learning and use: A sociocultural analysis. *Language and Education, 19*(1), 1–9.

Bartlett, L., & Holland, D. (2002). Theorizing the space of literacy practices. *Ways of Knowing, 2*(1), 10–22.

Barton, D. (1994). *Literacy: An Introduction to the Ecology of Written Language.* Oxford, UK: Blackwells.

Barton, D., & Hamilton, M. (1998). *Local literacies: Reading and writing in one community.* London: Routledge.

Bauman, Z. (2000). *Liquid modernity.* Cambridge, UK: Polity Press.

Baynham, M., & De Fina, A. (Eds.). (2005). *Dislocations/relocations: Narratives of dispacement.* Manchester, UK: St Jerome Publishing.

Bennett, T. (2005). Civic laboratories: Museums, cultural objecthood and the governance of the social. *Cultural Studies, 19*(5), 521–547.

Bird, V., & Pahl, K. (1994). Parent literacy in a community setting. *RaPAL Bulletin, 24,* 6–15.

Bissell, D. (2009). Inconsequential materialities: The movements of lost effects. *Space and Culture, 12*(1), 95–115.

Blackburn, M., & Clark, C. (Eds.). (2007). *Literacy research for political action and social change.* New York: Peter Lang.

Blommaert, J. (2008a). Bernstein and poetics revisited: Voice, globalization and education. *Discourse and Society, 19*(4), 425–451.

Blommaert, J. (2008b). Artefactual ideologies and the textual production of African languages. *Language & Communication, 28,* 291–307.

Bloome, D., Power Carter, S., Morton Christian, B., Madri, S., Otto, S., Suart-Faris, N., & Smith, M. (2008). *Discourse analysis in classrooms: Approaches to language and literacy research.* New York: Teachers College Press and National Conference on Research in Language and Literacy (NCRLL).

Bourdieu, P. (1990). *The logic of practice* (R. Nice, Trans.). Cambridge: Polity Press.

Bourdieu, P., & Wacquant, L. (1992). *Invitation to reflexive sociology.* Cambridge: Polity Press.

Brandt, D., & Clinton, K. (2002). The limits of the local: Expanding perspectives of literacy as a social practice. *Journal of Literacy Research, 34*(3), 337–356.

Brooke, R. E. (Ed.). (2003). *Rural voices: Place-conscious education and the teaching of writing.* New York: Teachers College Press.

Brooker, L. (2002). *Starting school: Young children learning cultures.* Milton Keynes, UK: Open University Press.

Burke, A., & Rowsell, J. (2008a). Assessing multimodal learning practice. *ELearning Journal.*

Burke, A., & Rowsell, J. (2008b). Screen pedagogy: Challenging perceptions of digital reading practice. *Changing English, 15*(4).

Carr, M. (2001). *Assessment in early childhood settings: Learning stories.* London: Sage.

Casey, E. (1996). How to get from space to place in a fairly short space of time. In S. Feld & K. Basso (Eds.), *Senses of place* (pp. 13–52). Santa Fe, NM: School of American Research Press.

Christiansen, P., Hockey, J., & James, A. (2001). Talk, silence and the material world: Patterns of indirect communication among agricultural families in northern England. In J. Hendry & C. W. Watson (Eds), *An Anthropology of Indirect Communication* (ASA Monograph No. 37, pp. 68–82). London: Routledge.

Christiansen, P., & O'Brien, M. (Eds.). (2003). *Children in the city: Home, neighbourhood and community.* London: Routledge.

Clark, E., Kjorholt, A. T., & Moss, P. (Eds.) (2005). *Beyond listening: Children's perspectives on early childhood services.* Bristol, UK: Policy Press.

Clifford, J. (1997). *Routes, travel and translation in the late twentieth century.* Cambridge, MA: Harvard University Press

Comber, B. (2010). Critical literacies in place: Teachers who work for just and sustainable communities. In J. Lavia & M. Moore (Eds.), *Cross-Cultural Perspectives in Policy and Practice: Decolonizing Community Contexts* (pp. 46–57). London: Routledge

Comber, B., Thompson, P., & Wells, M. (2001). Critical literacy finds a "place": Writing and social action in a neighborhood school. *Elementary School Journal, 101*(4), 451–464.

Connerton, P. (1989). *How societies remember.* Cambridge, UK: Cambridge University Press.

Cope, B., & Kalantzis, M. (Eds.). (2000). *Multiliteracies: The design of social futures.* London: Routledge.

Corbett, M. (2007). *Learning to leave: The irony of schooling in a coastal community.* Black Point, Nova Scotia: Fernwood Publishers.

Csikszentmihalyi, M., & Rochberg-Halton, E. (1981). *The meaning of things: Domestic objects and the self.* Cambridge, UK: Cambridge University Press.

Dewey, J., & Bentley, A. F. (1949). *Knowing and the known.* Westport, CT: Greenwood Press.

Dyson, A. H. (1993). *Social worlds of children learning to write in an urban primary school.* New York: Teachers College Press.

Dyson, A. H. (2003). *The brothers and sisters learn to write: Popular literacies in childhood and school cultures.* New York: Teachers College Press.

Edmondson, J. (2003). *Prairie town: Redefining rural life in the age of globalization.* Oxford, UK: Rowman & Littlefield.

Eisner, E. W. (2002). *The arts and the creation of mind.* New Haven, CT: Yale University Press.

Feiler, A., Andrews, J., Greenhough, P., Scanlan, M., Cin Lee, W., Johnson, D., & Hughes, M. (2007). *Improving primary literacy: Linking home and school.* London: Routledge.

Flewitt, R. (2008). Multimodal literacies. In J. Marsh & E. Hallet (Eds.), *Desirable literacies: Approaches to language and literacy in the early years* (pp. 122–139). London: Sage.

Gee, J. P. (2003). *What video games have to teach us about learning and literacy.* New York: Palgrave Macmillan.

Geertz, C. (1996). Afterword. In S. Feld & K. H. Basso (Eds.), *Sense of place* (pp. 259–262). Santa Fe, NM: School of American Research Press.

Georgakopoulou, A. (2007). Thinking big with small stories in narrative and identity analysis. In M. Bamberg (Ed.), *Narrative: State of the art* (pp. 145–154). Amsterdam: John Benjamins.

Giddens, A. (1991). *Modernity and self identity: Self and society in the late modern age.* Cambridge, UK: Polity Press.

Gonzalez, N., Moll, L., & Amanti, C. (Eds.). (2005). *Funds of knowledge: Theorizing practices in households, communities and classrooms.* Rahway, NJ: Erlbaum.

Green, J., & Bloome, D. (1997). Ethnography and ethnographers of and in education: A situated perspective. In J. Flood, S. Heath, & D. Lapp (Eds.), *A handbook for literacy educators: Research on teaching the communicative and visual arts* (pp. 1–12). New York: Macmillan.

Greenhough, P., Scanlan, M., Feiler, A., Johnson, D., Yee, W. C., Andrews, J., Price, A., Smithson, M., & Hughes, M. (2005). Boxing clever: Using shoeboxes to support home–school knowledge exchange. *Literacy, 39*(2), 97–103.

Gregory, E., Long, S., & Volk, D. (Eds.). (2004). *Many pathways to literacy: Young children learning with siblings, grandparents, peers, communities.* London: Routledge.

Gruenewald, D. (2003). The best of both worlds: A critical pedagogy of place. *Educational Researcher, 32*(4), 3–12.

Guitiérrez, K. (2009). *Syncretic literacies and ecologies in homes.* Paper presented at the annual meeting of the American Educational Research Association, San Diego, CA.

Guitiérrez, K., Baquedano-Lopez, P., & Tejada, C. (1999). Rethinking diversity: Hybridity and hybrid language practices in the third space. *Mind, Culture and Activity, 6*(4), 286–303.

Guitiérrez, K., & Stone, L. (2000). Synochronic and diachronic dimensions of social practice: An emerging methodology for cultural-historical perspectives on literacy learning. In C. Lee & P. Smagorinsky (Eds.), *Vygotskian perspectives on literacy research: Constructing meaning through collaborative inquiry* (pp. 150–165). New York: Cambridge University Press.

Heath, S. B. (1983). *Ways with words: Language, life and work in communities and classrooms.* Cambridge, UK: Cambridge University Press.

Heath, S. B., & Street, B. V. (with M. Mills). (2008). *On ethnography: Approaches to language and literacy research.* New York: Teachers College Press and National Conference on Research in Language and Literacy (NCRLL).

Herriot, J. (1976). *All creatures great and small.* London: Pan Macmillan. (Original work published 1970)

Herriot, J. (1978). *All things bright and beautiful.* London: Pan Macmillan. (Original work published 1973)

Hicks, D. (2002). *Reading lives: Working-class children and literacy learning.* New York: Teachers College Press

Holland, D., Lachicotte, W., Skinner, D., & Cain, C. (1998). *Identity and agency in cultural worlds.* Cambridge, MA: Harvard University Press.

Holland, D., & Leander, K. (2004). Ethnographic studies of positioning and subjectivity: An introduction. *Ethos, 32*, 127–130.

Homer. (1996). *The odyssey* (R. Fagles, Trans.). New York: Penguin.

Hoskins, J. (1998). *Biographical objects: How things tell the stories of people's lives.* London: Routledge.

Hurdley, R. (2006). Dismantling mantelpieces: Narrating identities and materializing culture in the home. *Sociology, 40*(4), 717–733.

Hymes, D. (Ed.). (1996). *Ethnography, linguistics, narrative inequality: Towards an understanding of voice.* London: Routledge.

Ingold, T. (2007). *Lines: A brief history.* London: Routledge.

Janks, H. (2000). Domination, access, diversity and design: A synthesis for critical literacy education. *Educational Review, 52*(2), 175–186.

Janks, H. (2010). *Literacy and power.* London: Routledge.

Jeffrey, B., & Troman, G. (2004). Time for Ethnography. *British Educational Research Journal, 30*(4), 536–548.

Jewitt, C., & Kress, G. (Eds.). (2003). *Multimodal literacy.* London: Peter Lang.

Keane, W. (2003). Semiotics and the social analysis of material things. *Language and Communication, 23*, 409–425.

Kell, C. (2006). Crossing the margins: Literacy, semiotics and the recontextualisation of meanings. In K. Pahl & J. Rowsell (Eds.), *Travel notes from the new literacy studies: Instances of practice* (pp. 147–172). Clevedon, UK: Multilingual Matters.

Kinloch, V. (2009). *Harlem on our minds: Place, race, and the literacies of urban youth.* New York: Teachers College Press.

Kress, G. (1997). *Before writing: Rethinking the paths to literacy.* London: Routledge.

Kress, G. (2003). *Literacy in the new media age.* London: Routledge.

Kress, G., & van Leeuwen, T. (1996). *Reading images: The grammar of visual design.* London: Routledge.

Lancaster, L. (2003). Beginning at the beginning: How a young child constructs time multimodally. In G. Kress & C. Jewitt (Eds.), *Multimodal literacy* (pp. 107–122). London: Peter Lang.

Langellier, K. M., & Peterson, E. E. (2004). *Storytelling in daily life.* Philadelphia: Temple University Press.

Lanigan, R. L. (1988). *Phenomenology of communication: Merleau-Ponty's thematic in communcology and semiology.* Pittsburgh, PA: Duquesne University Press.

Latour, B. (1987). *Science in action: How to follow scientists and engineers through society.* Cambridge: Harvard University Press.

Latour, B. (1994). On technical mediation: Philosophy, sociology, geneology. *Common Knowledge, 4,* 29–64.

Lave, J., & Wenger, E. (1991). *Situated learning: Legitimate peripheral participation.* Cambridge, UK: Cambridge University Press.

Lavia, J., & Moore, M. (Eds.). (2010). *Cross-cultural perspectives on policy and practice: Decolonizing community contexts.* London: Routledge.

Law, J. (1999). After ANT: Complexity, naming and topology. In J. Law & J. Hassard (Eds.), *Actor network theory and after* (pp. 1–15). Oxford, UK: Blackwell.

Law, J. (2003). *Materialities, spatialities, globalities.* Centre for Science Studies, Lancaster University.

Lawn, M., & Grosvenor, I. (Eds.). (2005). *Materialities of schooling: Design-technology-objects-routines.* Oxford, UK: Symposium Books.

Leander, K., & Sheehy, M. (Eds.). (2004). *Spatializing literacy research and practice.* New York: Berg.

Lee, C. D. (2008). The centrality of culture to the scientific study of learning and development: How an ecological framework in education research facilitates civic responsibility. *Educational Researcher, 37,* 267.

Lefebvre, H. (1991). *The production of space* (D. Nicholson-Smith, Trans.). Oxford, UK: Blackwell Publishing.

Lemke, J. (2000). Across the scales of time: Artifacts, activities, and meanings in ecosocial systems. *Mind, Culture, and Activity, 7*(4), 273–290.

Lipman, P. (2008). Mixed-income schools and housing: Advancing the neoliberal urban agenda. *Journal of Educational Policy, 23*(2), 119–134.

Macdonald, S. (2003). Museums, national, postnational and transcultural identities. *Museum and Society, 1*(1), 1–16.

McLean, C. (2008). *"Going back home": A narrative analysis of Caribbean adolescents' literacy practices.* Unpublished doctoral dissertation, University of Georgia.

Mathews, H. (2003). The street as liminal space: The barbed spaces of childhood. In P. Christiansen & M. O'Brien (Eds.), *Children in the city: Home, neighbourhood and community* (pp. 101–117). London: Routledge/Falmer.

Maybin, J. (2006). *Children's Voices: Talk, knowledge and identity.* Basingstoke, UK: Palgrave Macmillan.

Maybin, J. (2007). Literacy under and over the desk: Oppositions and heterogeneity. *Language and Education, 21*(6), 515–530.

Michael, M. (2004). On making data social: Heterogeneity in sociological practice. *Qualitative Research, 4*(5), 5–23.

Miller, D. (2008). *The comfort of things.* Cambridge, MA: Polity Press.

Moje, E. B. (2000). Circles of kinship, friendship, position, and power: Examining the community in community-based literacy research. *Journal of Literacy Research, 32*(1), 77–112.

Moje, E. B., Ciechanowski, K. M., Kramer, K., Ellis, L., Carrillo, R., & Collazo, T. (2004). Working toward third space in content area literacy: An examination of everyday funds of knowledge and discourse. *Reading Research Quarterly, 39*(1), 38–70.

Moll, L., Amanti, C., Neff, D., & Gonzalez, N. (1992). Funds of knowledge for teaching: Using a qualitative approach to connect homes and classrooms. *Theory into Practice, 31*, 132–141.

Murdoch, J. (1998). The spaces of actor-network theory. *Geoforum, 29*(4), 357–374.

Muspratt, S., Luke, A., & Freebody, P. (1997). *Constructing critical literacies.* Sydney: Allen & Unwin.

National Center for Education Studies. (2008). [Untitled document]. Retrieved April 7, 2010, from http://nces.ed.gov

Nelson, A. (2009). Storytelling and transformational learning. In B. Fisher-Yoshida, K. Dee Geller, & S. A. Schapiro (Eds.), *Innovations in transformative learning: Space, culture and the arts* (pp. 207–222). New York: Peter Lang.

Neuman, S., & Celano, D. (2001). Access to print in low-income and middle-income communities: An ecological study of four neighbourhoods. *Reading Research Quarterly, 36*(1), 8–26.

Nichols, S., Nixon, H., & Rowsell, J. (2009). Shaping the identities and practices in relation to early years literacy. *Literacy, 43*(2), 65–74.

Obama, B. (1995). *Dreams from my father.* New York: Three Rivers Press.

Orellana, M. F. (1999). Space and place in an urban landscape: Learning from children's views of their social worlds. *Visual Sociology, 14*, 23–88.

Orlove, B. S. (1980). Ecological anthropology. *Annual Review of Anthropology, 9*, 235–273.

Pahl, K. (1999). *Transformations: Children's meaning making in a nursery.* Stoke on Trent, UK: Trentham Books.

Pahl, K. (2002). Ephemera, mess and miscellaneous piles: Texts and practices in families. *Journal of Early Childhood Literacy, 2*(2), 145–165.

Pahl, K. (2003). Children's text making at home: Transforming meaning across modes. In C. Jewitt & G. Kress (Eds.), *Multimodal literacy* (pp. 139–154). New York: Peter Lang.

Pahl, K. (2004). Narratives, artifacts and cultural identities: An ethnographic study of communicative practices in homes. *Linguistics and Education, 15*(4), 339–358.

Pahl, K. (2005). Children's popular culture in the home: Tracing cultural practices in texts. In J. Marsh & E. Millard (Eds.), *Popular literacies, childhood and schooling* (pp. 29–53). London: Routledge/Falmer.

Pahl, K. (2006). An inventory of traces: Children's photographs of their toys in three London homes. *Visual Communication, 5*(1), 95–114.

Pahl, K. (2007a). Creativity in events and practices: A lens for understanding children's multimodal texts. *Literacy, 41*(2), 86–92.

Pahl, K. (2007b). Timescales and ethnography: Understanding a child's meaning-making across three sites: A home, a classroom and a family literacy class. *Ethnography and Education, 2*(2), 175–190.

Pahl, K. (2008). Tracing habitus in texts and practices. In A. Luke & J. Albright (Eds.), *Pierre Bourdieu and literacy education* (pp. 187–208). London: Routledge.

Pahl, K. (2009). Interactions, intersections and improvisations: Studying the multimodal texts and classroom talk of six to seven year olds. *Journal of Early Childhood Literacy, 9*(2), 188–210.

Pahl, K. (2010). Changing literacies: Schools, communities and homes. In J. Lavia & M. Moore (Eds.), *Cross-cultural perspectives on policy and practice: Decolonizing community contexts* (pp. 58–71). London: Routledge.

Pahl, K., & Macdonald, S. (2008). *Translating objects.* Unpublished grant proposal to the Arts and Humanities Research Council, UK.

Pahl, K., & Pollard, A. (2008). "Bling—the Asians introduced that to the country": Gold and its value within a group of families of South Asian origin in Yorkshire. *Visual Communication, 7*(2), 170–182.

Pahl, K. with Pollard, A., & Rafiq, Z. (2009). Changing identities, changing spaces: The Ferham Families exhibition in Rotherham. *Moving Worlds, 9*(2), 80–103.

Pahl, K., & Rowsell, J. (2005). *Literacy and education: The new literacy studies in the classroom.* London: Paul Chapman.

Pahl, K., & Rowsell, J. (Eds.). (2006). *Travel notes from the new literacy studies: Instances of practice.* Clevedon, UK: Multilingual Matters.

Pahl, R., & Spencer, L. (2003). *Personal communities: Not simply families of 'fate' or 'choice'* (Working Papers of the Institute for Social and Economic Research, No. 2003,4). Colchester, UK: University of Essex.

Pink, S. (2007). *Doing visual ethnography* (2nd ed.). London: Sage.

Pink, S. (2008). An urban tour: An ethnography of contemporary sense-making. *Ethnography, 9*(2), 175–196.

Pink, S. (2009). *Doing sensory ethnography.* London: Sage

Rampton, B. (2006). *Language in late modernity.* Cambridge, UK: Cambridge University Press.

Rogers, R., Mosley, M., Kramer, M. A., & the Literacy for Social Justice Teacher Research Group. (2009). *Designing socially just learning communities.* London: Routledge.

Rogers, R., & O'Brien, D. (in press). Parental involvement with a purpose: Get the lead out! In S. Greene & C. Compton-Lilly (Eds.), *Family literacy: Complexities, concerns, considerations.* New York: Teachers College Press.

Rogoff, B. (2003). *The cultural nature of human development.* Cambridge, UK: Cambridge University Press.

Rosowsky, A. (2001). Decoding as a cultural practice and its effects on the reading process of bilingual pupils. *Language and Education, 15*(1), 56–70.

Rosowsky, A. (2008). *Heavenly readings: Liturgical literacy in a multilingual context.* Bristol, UK: Multilingual Matters.

Rowsell, J. (2003a). The production-reception continuum: Activating publishing practices during literacy events. *Changing English, 10,* 59–71.

Rowsell, J. (2003b). Semiotic consciousness in educational textbooks. *International Journal of Applied Semiotics, 4*(2), 43–63.

Rowsell, J. (2003c). Identities in progress: Towards a notion of modified habitus. *Ways of Knowing*, 1(1), 3–15.

Rowsell, J. (2006a). Corporate Crossings: Tracing textual crossings. In K. Pahl & J. Rowsell (Eds.), *Travel notes from the new literacy studies* (pp. 195–219). Clevedon, UK: Multilingual Matters.

Rowsell, J. (2006b). *Family literacy experiences: Creating reading and writing opportunities for student achievement*. Markham: Pembroke Publishing.

Rowsell, J. (2008). Improvising on artistic habitus: Sedimenting identity into art. In J. Albright & A. Luke (Eds.), *Literacy and Bourdieu* (pp. 325–346). Mahway, NJ: Lawrence Erlbaum.

Rowsell, J. (2009). Artifactual literacy. In M. Hagood (Ed.), *New literacies: Learning from youth in out-of-school and in-school contexts* (pp. 65–80). New York: Routledge.

Rowsell, J., & Booth, D. (2005). Introduction. In J. Rowsell & D. Booth (Eds.), *Literacy revisited* (Vol. 6). Toronto: OISE/University of Toronto Press.

Rowsell, J., & Pahl, K. (2007). Sedimented identities in texts: Instances of practice. *Reading Research Quarterly*, 42(3), 388–401.

Rowsell, J., & Rajaratnam, D. (2005). There is no place like home: A teacher perspective on literacies across educational contexts. In B. Street (Ed.), *Literacies across educational contexts* (pp. 233–251). Philadelphia: Caslon Publishing.

Rowsell, J., Sztainbok, V., & Blaney, J. (2007). 'Losing strangeness': Using culture to mediate ESL teaching. *Language, Culture and Identity*, 20(2), 63–91.

Salinger, J. D. (1951). *The catcher in the rye*. New York: Penguin.

Samuel, R., & Thompson, P. (Eds.). (1990). *The myths we live by*. London: Routledge.

Sanchez, P. (2007). Cultural authenticity and transnational Latina youth: Constructing a metanarrative across borders. *Linguistics and Education*, 18, 258–282.

Saxena, M. (2000). Taking account of history and culture in community-based research on multilingual literacy. In M. Martin-Jones & K. Jones (Eds.), *Multilingual literacies* (pp. 273–275). Amsterdam: John Benjamins.

Scanlan, M. (2008). *My story in a box: Linking home and school to explore identity, creativity, writing and oracy*. Unpublished doctoral dissertation, University of Bristol, Bristol, UK.

Schultz, K. (2003). *Listening: A framework for teaching across differences*. New York: Teachers College Press.

Scollon, R., & Scollon, S. (2003). *Discourses in place: Language in the material world*. London: Routledge.

Sennett, R., & Cobb, J. (1973). *The hidden injuries of class*. New York: Knopf.

Sheridan, M. P., & Rowsell, J. (2010). *Design literacies: Learning and innovation in the digital age*. London: Routledge.

Shuman, A. (2007). Entitlement and empathy in personal narrative. In M. Bamberg (Ed.), *Narrative: State of the art* (pp. 175–184). Amsterdam: John Benjamins.

Stein, P. (2003). The Olifantsvlei fresh stories project: Multimodality, creativity and fixing in the semiotic chain. In C. Jewitt & G. Kress (Eds.), *Multimodal literacy* (pp. 123–138). New York: Peter Lang.

Street, B. V. (1984). *Literacy in theory and practice*. Cambridge, UK: Cambridge University Press.

Street, B. V. (Ed.). (1993). *Cross-cultural approaches to literacy.* Cambridge, UK: Cambridge University Press.

Street, B. V. (2008). New literacies, new times: Developments in literacy studies. In B. V. Street & N. Hornberger (Eds.), *Encyclopedia of language and education: Vol. 2. Literacy* (pp. 3–14). New York: Springer.

Street, B. V. (2009). *"Hidden" features of academic paper writing* (Working Papers in Educational Linguistics). Philadelphia: University of Pennsylvania.

Street, B. V., & Street, J. (1991). The schooling of literacy. In D. Barton & R. Ivanic (Eds.), *Writing in the community* (pp. 143–166). London: Sage.

Thompson, P. (2008). Learning Through Extended Talk. *Language and Education, 22*(3), 241–257.

Tuhiwai Smith, L. (1999). *Decolonizing methodologies: Research and indigenous people.* London: Zed Books.

Turkle, S. (1984). *The second self: Computers and the human spirit.* New York: Simon and Schuster.

Turkle, S. (2007). *Evocative objects: Things we think with.* Cambridge, MA: MIT Press.

Van-der-Vord, M. (2008). A community centre's cultural influence within the classroom: Place, third spaces and identities. Unpublished master's thesis, University of Sheffield, UK.

Vygotsky, L. S. (1978). *Mind in society: The development of higher psychological processes.* M. Cole, V. John-Steiner, S. Scribner, & E. Souberman (Eds.). Cambridge, MA: Harvard University Press.

Watson, M. (2008). *MLA generic social outcomes (GSOs) case study: Calderdale MBC.* Unpublished manuscript.

Watson, N., & Cunningham-Burley, S. (Eds.). (2001). *Reframing the body.* Basingstoke, UK: Palgrave Macmillan.

Whitty, P., & Rose, S., with Baisley, D., Comeau, L., & Thompson, A. (2008). Honouring educators' co-construction of picture books. *Child Study, 33*(2), 21–23.

Wilhelm, B. (2003). "Common threads": A writing curriculum centered in our place. In R. E. Brooke (Ed.), *Rural voices: Place-conscious education and the teaching of writing* (pp. 83–101). New York: Teachers College Press.

Williams, R. (1958). *Culture and society: 1780–1950.* London: Chatto & Windus.

Williams, R. (1961). *The long revolution.* London: Chatto & Windus.

Williams, R. (1989). *Resources of hope: Culture, democracy, socialism.* London: Verso.

Winnicott, D.W. (1971). *Playing and reality.* Routledge: London.

Woolf, V. (1977). *To the lighthouse.* London: Grafton Books. (Original work published 1927)

Wortham, S. (2001). *Narratives in action: A strategy for research and analysis.* New York: Teachers College Press.

Wright, R. (1945). *Black boy.* New York: Bantam.

About the Authors

KATE PAHL is a Senior Lecturer in Education in the Department of Educational Studies at the University of Sheffield. She obtained her MA in Literacies in Education at the Institute of Education, London, and her PhD at King's College, University of London. Kate's research centers on ways in which families use literacy in everyday contexts. She is interested in intergenerational family stories and in ways of using these to create learning resources in family literacy contexts. She is particularly interested in the relationship between narratives of migration and artifacts in homes. She works with museums, libraries, and arts organizations together with schools to create and research links between the arts and literacy. She is currently involved in a 2-year community literacy study, for Inspire Rotherham, an initiative designed to raise literacy aspirations, funded by Yorkshire Forward. Previous publications with Jennifer Rowsell include *Literacy and Education: The New Literacy Studies in the Classroom* (Paul Chapman, 2005) and *Travel Notes from the New Literacy Studies* (Multilingual Matters, 2006). Kate directs the Working with Communities master's course and also teaches in the literacy and language strand of the doctoral program and the online MA in New Literacies at the Department of Educational Studies, University of Sheffield.

JENNIFER ROWSELL is an Associate Professor of Literacy Education and Canada Research Chair in Multiliteracies at Brock University in Canada. She obtained her Certificate in the Teaching of English as a Foreign Language from Rutgers University in Paris, her master's in comparative literature at University College, London, and her PhD in literacy education at King's College, University of London. Jennifer's research centers on ways in which K–12 students can think, work, and design in multimodal and artifactual ways. She is interested in ways of rethinking literacy so that there is a better match between in-school and out-of-school models of literacy, which involves work in the domains of early-childhood education, family literacy, and adolescent literacy. She is currently involved in three research studies: Artifactual English, a study of adolescence and multimodality; a multisite ecological study in Australia and the United States with Sue Nichols, Helen Nixon, and Sophie Rainbird of the University of South Australia; and an international study of intergenerational family stories. Her publications with Kate Pahl include *Literacy and Education: The New Literacy Studies in the Classroom* (Paul Chapman, 2005), *Travel Notes from the New Literacy Studies: Instances of Practice* (Multilingual Matters, 2006), and *Family Literacy Experiences* (Pembroke, 2006); with Mary P. Sheridan, she published *Design Literacies: Learning and Innovation in the Digital Age* (Routledge, 2010). Jennifer coordinates the English Education program at Rutgers Graduate School of Education.

Index

Note: Page numbers followed by f and t refer to figures and tables respectively.